CHOCOCO
chocolate cookbook

CHOCOCO
chocolate cookbook

Claire Burnet   Photography by Jonathan Gregson

RYLAND
PETERS
& SMALL
LONDON NEW YORK

Dedication
To Mum, you inspired my love of food
and chocolate. This is for you. x

Senior designer Megan Smith
Commissioning editor Julia Charles
Production Gordana Simakovic
Art director Leslie Harrington
Publishing director Alison Starling

Food stylist Joss Herd
Prop stylist Liz Belton
Indexer Hilary Bird
**Chococo logo, branding, and
packaging design** Pearlfisher

First published in the United States
in 2011 by Ryland Peters & Small, Inc.
519 Broadway, 5th Floor
New York, NY 10012
www.rylandpeters.com

10 9 8 7 6 5 4 3 2 1

Text © Claire Burnet 2011
Chococo ® is a registered trademark
of Chococo: The Purbeck Chocolate Co.
Design and photographs
© Ryland Peters & Small 2011

ISBN: 978-1-84975-092-9

Printed and bound in China

Notes
• All spoon measurements are level,
unless otherwise specified.
• Ovens should be preheated to the
specified temperature. Recipes in this book
were tested using a regular oven. If using a
convection oven, follow the manufacturer's
instructions for adjusting temperatures.
• All eggs are extra-large, unless otherwise
specified and we recommend that you
choose organic free-range eggs. Recipes
containing raw or partially-cooked egg,
should not be served to the very young,
very old, anyone with a compromised
immune system, or pregnant women.
• When using the grated peel of citrus fruit
in a dish, try to find organic or unwaxed
fruits and wash well before using. If you
can find only treated fruit, scrub well in
warm soapy water and rinse before using.

CONTENTS

The **CHOCOCO** story

Chococo, the Purbeck Chocolate Company, was set up by me and my husband Andy in 2002 for one simple reason, my love of chocolate. I first started cooking with chocolate as a child when making Christmas treats with my foodie mum, and I discovered the world of fine chocolate when exploring Belgium and France while my parents lived in Brussels in the mid 1980s. Artisan chocolates handmade with fresh cream ganache fillings, created to be eaten within days, were a revelation, as were Continental chocolate bars with more cocoa solids and less sugar than their British cousins, and with no added vegetable fats. Proper chocolate became a constant in my life, long before the creation of Chococo; parties usually involved a chocolate dessert or fondue, and when we got married, our guests tucked into ice cream sundaes and our wedding cake was chocolate!

I am evangelical about chocolate, both as a consumer and as a chocolate maker. I believe that it's all about the balance of flavors, and that pure food freshly made with real, seasonal ingredients you have in your kitchen, will always taste more sublime than a concoction using ingredients straight out of a chemistry lab. And that, simply, is what Chococo is all about. Taking the leap to set up our own business, in a Dorset seaside town on England's south coast, was a complete career and life change, created out of my vision to make fresh chocolates, using not "Belgian" chocolate, but origin chocolate, produced from "fine flavor" cocoa beans processed into "couverture" chocolate in its country of origin.

In fact, I think we were one of the first, if not *the* first, regional British chocolate maker to focus on making truly fresh chocolates and when we say fresh we mean it. Made daily with no additives or preservatives, our creations are pure blends of fine chocolate with fresh cream and natural flavorings, so that our customers can discover the joy of tasting such chocolates.

We also work with as many locally sourced, seasonal ingredients as possible. It makes sense to us—the food is fresher, has traveled less and we are supporting our local economy. It's also great fun to work with producers who are as passionate about their cows, bees, or hedgerows as we are about our chocolates! Dorset has many wonderful and thriving food-based businesses. We are very proud to be part of that world and honored to have won so many awards, for both our chocolates and our business ethos, in both regional and national competitions.

Since we established Chococo, our range of services has grown alongside our range of chocolates. As well as offering an online mail order service and supplying premium retailers, we also have a chocolate café next to our shop at "Cocoa Central", in Swanage, Dorset and run chocolate workshops for kids of all ages from our original chocolate kitchen opposite.

With this book, I want to share with you my passion for chocolate as well as introduce you to the spirit of Chococo. As such, I have incorporated the flavors of many of our award-winning chocolates in these recipes and some are my interpretations of classic desserts, which I have given the Chococo treatment—full of flavor, color, and joy! I have also strived to ensure that the recipes are easy to make, use accessible, seasonal ingredients, and require only basic kitchen equipment, the most complex being a handheld electric mixer.

I hope that this book inspires you to get creative in your kitchen and delight your family and friends, even if it is as simple as rustling up a batch of chocolate chunk cookies or muffins to eat warm with a cup of foaming hot chocolate... enjoy!

Claire

WORKING WITH CHOCOLATE

A BRIEF BACKGROUND

"There is no love more sincere than the love of chocolate." This is one of my favorite chocolate quotes. How true that sentiment is, from the Mayan and Aztec Mesoamerican cultures, for whom cacao played such a central role in their culture, to the Spanish conquistadors who brought cacao beans back to Europe in the early 16th century and introduced the Spanish aristocracy to the concept of drinking cacahuatl. Over time, sugar and milk were added and as technology advanced, so did the chocolate makers' abilities to process chocolate into the myriad of forms we know and love today.

However, over the course of the 20th century, much chocolate suffered at the hands of large commercial manufacturers who smothered it in sugar (and in some cases added vegetable fat), and educated consumers to think of chocolate as a very sweet and cheap confection with no sense at all of its story from pod to palette. We run chocolate-making demonstrations regularly here at Chococo, complete with dried cocoa pods and beans and for many of our customers, it is a revelation to hear that chocolate grows on trees!

This book is all about making delicious recipes for you and your family and friends to enjoy at home rather than a treatise on fine chocolate but hopefully this potted summary will give you a glimpse into this fascinating world.

WHERE DOES COCOA COME FROM?

Theobroma cacao (the botanical name for the cocoa tree) is indigenous to the Amazon basin area of northern South America. There is much debate in learned circles about exactly how it spread to Central America, where it became so important to the Mesoamerican civilizations in what is now Mexico, Guatemala, and Belize. Cocoa cultivation, driven primarily by colonization, has spread to hot, humid countries up to 68°F either side of the equator and it is now grown in Central and South America, the Caribbean, West Africa, Tanzania, Madagascar, Indonesia, Malaysia, and Vietnam.

WHAT DOES THE COCOA TREE LOOK LIKE?

It is quite a small under-storey rainforest tree, requiring constant heat, high humidity, and shade, but is very distinctive as its fruit, the cocoa pods, grow off the tree trunk as well as along the branches. Different varieties of cocoa trees will yield pods of different shapes, sizes, and colors when ripe, with their 30–50 cocoa beans nestled inside, surrounded by an edible, sweet white flesh, which by the way, is quite delicious!

BUT CHOCOLATE'S JUST CHOCOLATE ISN'T IT?

When we run our chocolate-making demonstrations here at Chococo, I always ask our visitors about their wine choices of years ago and we all chuckle about those bottles celebrating towers of black and religious

ladies in blue and then I ask them about their wine preferences of today...

If you start thinking of chocolate as being like fine wine or coffee, where we take for granted the mind-boggling varieties of grape and bean varieties, processing methods, and countries of origin as factors that influence the taste of the final product, the world of chocolate will suddenly come alive. You will start looking at it in a new light and that "industrial" chocolate that you once thought of as chocolate, will never have quite the same appeal again. When you put a piece of fine dark chocolate in your mouth and focus on the flavors that start to sing as it melts, you will become aware of various floral, nutty, spicy, earthy, fruity, or toasty flavor profiles and, as you try different chocolates, you will notice the distinct differences in flavors between them. To give you a brief overview, there are three main cocoa bean types. Two are known as the "fine flavor" grades of criollo and trinitario, which account for up to only 15 percent of total world production. Within these types you can discover the finest chocolate in the world, from the rare chao and porcelana from Venezuela, to rich, fruity trinitarios from Madagascar, Grenada, and other delicious single origin bean types from Central America, Peru, Bolivia, and others.

The final main bean type is the forestero. Although originally from the Amazon basin, this bean type being more robust (but arguably more acidic and less delicate in flavor), provides the bulk of total world cocoa production today, mostly from West Africa. *But*, and this is an important but, the flavor of your chocolate is not dictated purely by the bean. It will also be influenced by other key factors including the "terroir" in which the trees are grown, how the beans are harvested and processed from tree to bar, and also how the weather affects harvests year on year.

SO HOW ARE COCOA BEANS HARVESTED?
By hand. Every cocoa pod is cut off its tree with a knife. This cannot be mechanized and the harvesting of cocoa is totally manual, in contrast with the industrial processes used to process dried beans into chocolate. The pods are split open and the beans and their sweet flesh are scooped out.

WHAT HAPPENS NEXT?
This is the bit that I think surprises people the most. Chocolate is effectively a slow food as it takes ideally two weeks to prepare cocoa beans to a point where a chocolate maker can then process them into chocolate. The first stage of the process after harvesting the beans is fermentation. Fresh wet beans are placed in piles on the ground, or in cans, and left covered with jute and banana leaves to ferment for up to eight days. As the beans heat up, the sweet flesh ferments and liquefies and enzymes are activated within the beans that will release chocolate flavors when they are roasted. Rush the fermentation process and you will adversely affect the flavor of the eventual chocolate. The beans are then dried, ideally in the sun for a week, to reduce the moisture content down to six and seven percent.

Given that cocoa grows in equatorial regions, cocoa is often dried on racks on wheels so that the beans can be quickly rolled under cover when it rains.

HOW ARE DRIED BEANS PROCESSED INTO CHOCOLATE?

Approximately 3.5 million tonnes of cocoa are produced each year and most dried cocoa beans are exported to Europe or the USA for processing into chocolate. There are a few exceptions to this and we at Chococo are big supporters of chocolate that is turned from bean to bar in its country of origin, thereby also adding value to their local economies far more than by exporting raw cocoa beans. Some of these exceptions include El Rey from Venezuela, Pacari from Ecuador, the delicious bars by the Grenada Chocolate Company, which are increasingly widely available in supermarkets in North America, Luker from Colombia, El Ceibo from Bolivia, and Madecasse from Madagascar.

To process beans into chocolate, they are roasted (this is a critical stage as it is very easy to ruin beans by over-roasting), then winnowed to remove the shells and chopped into nibs. Roasted cocoa nibs are quite delicious to eat. Intense, nutty (and not at all sweet), they are becoming more widely available and are delicious used in bars and cookies and sprinkled on ice cream: you will find some recipes in this book using cocoa nibs.

The nibs are then ground in a *mélangeur* to form a paste known as cocoa mass or liquor. In the main, this liquor is then pressed to extract the fat, known as cocoa butter, to leave a dry cake residue, which after further processing to reduce its acidity, is cocoa powder.

Most of the flavor of chocolate is in the powder, the melting property of chocolate is in the butter. Cocoa butter's low melting point is highly sought after by the cosmetics and pharmaceutical industries but, as they don't want a highly flavored fat, most cocoa butter is deodorized (effectively steam cleaned), which results in a very inert white fat with very little flavor. However this deodorized cocoa butter is also used in the chocolate industry to make most white chocolates.

Depending on the desired chocolate, cocoa mass, and extra cocoa butter (described on packaging as cocoa solids) are then mixed with sugar to make dark chocolate, or with both sugar and milk powder to make semi-sweet or milk chocolate. While white chocolate is a blend of just the cocoa butter with milk and sugar. These different substances are then blended together for up to several days in a process called "conching." This penultimate element of the production process refines the textures and flavors to create a smooth liquid ready for tempering. Finally, this liquid is tempered (see page 12 for an explanation of this term) and moulded into its final form ready for consumption.

Professional chocolate makers work with "couverture" chocolate, which contains a higher percentage of cocoa butter to give chocolate more shine, but widely available good-quality chocolate will work perfectly well for making all of the recipes in this book. I have specified a cocoa solid percentage for guidance where appropriate.

WHAT CHOCOLATE TO BUY

Most of my recipes require a dark chocolate of ideally 65–70% cocoa solids. However, do be aware that just stating 70% on a bar is not a guarantee of quality. You need to judge the chocolate on more than just its ratio of chocolate to sugar. In terms of the percentage of cocoa solids, think of it as a guide. As a generalization, less than 65% cocoa solids in a dark bar and sugar starts to take over in terms of taste, while dark chocolate with a cocoa solids content much higher than 75–80% can be overpowering in flavor and require significantly more sugar to make it palatable. Although I have not specified chocolate of particular origin for most of these recipes, when buying chocolate to cook with, look out for the increasingly widely available good-quality dark chocolate bars whose labels describe not only the percentage of cocoa solids, but also ideally the bean type(s), the country of origin, the terroir, the producer, and any flavor notes that you might expect to find. If so, you are more likely to enjoy a chocolate with more integrity and depth of flavor than a mass-produced bar, and you can start to discover flavors that you like to work with in your chocolate cooking at home.

For a real treat, look out for chocolate by specialist "bean to bar" producers such as El Ceibo, Madecasse, Original Beans, Amedei, Michel Cluisel, Bernachon, Pralus, Mast Brothers, Askinosie, and Amano among others, available in more specialist shops or through websites. However, if you feel that these beautiful, and rightly pricey, artisan chocolates are best discovered and savored as they are, rather than being cooked with,

I couldn't disagree with you! With regard to milk and semi-sweet chocolates, do buy bars with more than 30% cocoa solids, ideally they should have a minimum of 35%. Any less and there just isn't enough cocoa in the bar to be contributing any flavor! This is a personal plea as I am constantly horrified at how unnecessarily sweet so many commercial milk chocolates are, which just perpetuates the impression that chocolate is a very sweet product.

And finally, to white chocolate. As previously described, most white chocolate is made with deodorized cocoa butter so lacks aroma and flavor. We work with a very unusual natural un-deodorized white chocolate and this may become a trend. In the meantime, look out for bars containing ideally about 30% cocoa butter and no added vegetable fat. Another mission of mine is to persuade people to stop giving white chocolate to small children. Contrary to popular belief, it is not better for them and just educates palettes at a young age to think of chocolate as being very sweet. It is far better to give little people good-quality milk, or better still, dark chocolate.

WHAT CHOCOLATE NOT TO BUY

Avoid any chocolate low in cocoa solids and containing vegetable fat in addition to cocoa butter. It will be declared on the back of packaging, is not pure chocolate and won't behave properly when you cook with it. Also avoid any chocolate containing vanillin rather than natural vanilla—it is a cheap substitute for the real thing. A final thought is for vegans or anyone intolerant to dairy. Please do not assume that all dark chocolate is free from dairy. Some brands add a small percentage of milk powder to their dark chocolate bars but it will be declared on the back label.

WORKING WITH CHOCOLATE AT HOME

This most beloved of confections has a reputation for being high maintenance, but as long as you respect it, focus on it and pay attention to the weather (yes you did read that correctly!) you should be able to create delicious chocolate creations without dramas.

Chocolate is demanding in that it doesn't like extremes. It doesn't like to get too hot (an ideal working environment temperature is around 68°F), or too cold and it certainly doesn't like high humidity, so avoid tempering chocolate on very wet days, very cold days or during heatwaves! You will be surprised at how hot and humid your kitchen can get if you are doing a lot of cooking, or by simply putting the kettle on, so think about the environmental conditions before embarking on any chocolate work.

Ideally after working with chocolate, you would put it in a cool dry space of 58°F to set. If you can put your chocolate creation in a pantry, unheated room, or garage, perfect, but if the only cool space is a fridge, be aware of what else is in it. Try to keep your chocolate away from any strong odors in there and once it has set, keep it in a sealed airtight container to keep the moisture out.

STORING YOUR CHOCOLATE BEFORE USE

A good chocolate cook will always have a stash of chocolate ready for use at a moment's notice, and preferably hidden away from prying eyes. Store your chocolate in a cool, dark, dry place, well wrapped, or in an airtight container, so that it cannot absorb moisture or smells from other items around it.

MELTING CHOCOLATE

The secret is to melt chocolate slowly and not to overheat it. You don't want to let the chocolate reach a temperature in excess of 113°F ideally, but it is surprisingly easy to do so if you get distracted and do not pay attention to it. I am not a fan of melting chocolate in the microwave as I think it is too easy for it to melt unevenly and to burn the chocolate. For best results, I always recommend using a heatproof glass bowl, so that you can see the water underneath, which sits snugly over a saucepan filled with water to an inch in depth. The water must not touch the base of the bowl and be barely simmering. Do not be tempted to rush the process by letting the water reach a boil; if you overheat your chocolate, it will go grainy. It is also vital that you do not allow any water to come into contact with the chocolate as it will seize, which means solidify. If you are melting only a small amount of chocolate (less than 4 oz.), turn the heat off once the water has warmed to a simmer, and there should be enough residual heat under the bowl to melt all of the chocolate. Whenever you do melt chocolate in a bowl set over a saucepan, once it has melted and a recipe says to take it off the heat, actually remove the bowl from the pan of water, not just the pan from the heat.

TEMPERING CHOCOLATE

This, as they say, is "the science bit" and should help to explain why chocolate sometimes just doesn't work as you expect it to! You will come across lots of chocolate recipes that require you not only to melt the chocolate but also to "temper" it to make a finished creation with a pleasing snap and shine. Tempering takes the chocolate through a specific, and quite narrow, temperature curve to ensure that it is at the correct crystaline structure to work with. The rule of thumb for dark chocolate is from 113°F down to 84–86°F and back up to about 91°F. Milk, semi-sweet, and white chocolates have slightly lower temperature profiles but just to make it all more complicated, tempering profiles will vary slightly from chocolate to chocolate, due primarily to variations in the amount of cocoa butter used by different producers. It can be easy to get the tempering process wrong and even though the chocolate looks fine to work with in its liquid state, it "blooms", appearing grey and streaky and has no snap when it sets.

The classic artisan method for tempering chocolate involves pouring melted chocolate onto a marble slab,

swirling it around to cool it and then returning it to a bowl. However, this process may not be that practical for a domestic cook as it requires a large marble slab, ideally a minimum of 2 lbs. of chocolate to work with and is also very messy!

SEED TEMPERING

This is a more practical option and how I temper chocolate when working with smaller quantities. If you have a digital thermometer even better, but you can do this without one. The rule of thumb with seed tempering is that you melt about 70 percent of your required chocolate and then "seed" the remaining 30 percent to help achieve the correct crystaline structure as you take the chocolate through the temperature curve.

Step 1: Melt 70 percent of your chopped chocolate very slowly in a bowl set over a saucepan of barely simmering water, not letting the base of the bowl touch the water. Do not let the chocolate go above 113°F ideally for dark chocolate or 104°F for milk, semi-sweet, or white chocolate.

Step 2: Once the chocolate has melted, take the bowl off the pan, place the bowl on a cool surface, add the remaining chopped chocolate. Stir with a rubber spatula to melt it in and cool the chocolate down to about 84–86°F. Milk and white chocolate can go down to 82°F. The chocolate will thicken as it cools. You can also check that the chocolate has cooled down by placing a little on your lower lip. It shouldn't feel hot or cold to the touch.

Step 3: Finally, put your bowl of chocolate back on the saucepan and stir to bring the temperature back up to 91–93°F using the residual heat from the water in the saucepan. As it warms it should become slightly thinner and you can double check whether your chocolate is tempered by placing a thin layer of chocolate onto a palette knife and putting it in the freezer. Once set, if it breaks with a snap and has a good shine underneath, you have tempered chocolate!

WORKING WITH TEMPERED CHOCOLATE

Once you are happy that your chocolate is tempered, you will need to work fast. It is cooling all the time that you are working with it and by definition, is going out of temper. If you notice that your chocolate is thickening significantly as you are working with it, pop it back onto the saucepan of warm water and give it a gentle warming for just a couple of minutes.

WHAT TO DO IF THINGS GO WRONG

At the melting stage: If you realize that you have overheated the chocolate, leave it to cool completely and start all over again. If water gets into it, it will thicken, or "seize" to use the technical term, and you can rescue chocolate only by adding more water and effectively making a sauce. You can use this for sauces or in baking but not to temper with.

After it has set: If it blooms, at some point the chocolate was possibly out of temper when you were working with it. Alternatively, it could be that when

setting, it was left in too warm a place, so has taken too long to set, or conversely has got too cold (I told you it was fussy!).

Bloom will affect its appearance and mouthfeel but not its taste. If appropriate, sift confectioners' sugar or cocoa powder over the surface just before serving to hide a multitude of sins, as my mum would say. Alternatively, you can also hide problems by covering a surface with chocolate curls (see right) or drizzling more chocolate over the top, either by using a teaspoon or with a homemade piping bag (see below).

HOW TO MAKE A PIPING BAG

This is easier to make than it sounds but you might need to practise it before you start melting your chocolate! It will enable you to decorate truffles, cookies or cakes, and also create a number of different chocolate shapes.

Cut an isosceles triangle from baking parchment about 16 inches on its long side and 12 inches on its two shorter sides.

Looking at the triangle as if it is a mountain, take the bottom right hand point and curl it towards you as you take it to meet the mountain top. Then, while holding that piece in place, take the left-hand point and wrap it around the outside to meet the other piece at the back of the mountain tip.

You should now have a pointed cone with the two edges meeting at the back, which you can fold over to secure the cone ready for filling.

HOW TO USE YOUR PIPING BAG

Lay a sheet of baking parchment or rigid cellophane film onto a baking sheet and half fill the piping bag with tempered chocolate. Fold the sides of the bag into the center, turn it over several times from the top to prevent any chocolate escaping (this will also force the chocolate towards the tip) and snip a small hole in the end with scissors. To pipe, hold the bag between your thumb and forefinger as you would a pen. You can make simple lattice shapes, squiggles, swirls and, with a little practice, even pipe your name either freehand or by tracing over a pattern that you have placed under the cellophane. Leave to set in a cool place and store in an airtight container until required.

TO MAKE CHOCOLATE CURLS

Temper 4 oz. of chocolate by the seed tempering method (see page 14) and pour a thin layer over a cold surface, either a marble surface if you have one, or the back of a baking sheet. Leave in a cool place until almost set. Drag the blade of a large sharp knife at a 45° angle across the chocolate to make the curls. If the knife sinks into the chocolate, it needs more time to set. If the chocolate is too hard, leave it at room temperature for a few minutes to soften slightly before starting again. Put your curls on baking parchment in an airtight container in a cool place until needed. If this method seems too fiddly for you, you can simply use a cheese grater to create little curls or drag a knife across the back of a bar of chocolate for thinner shards that will still look effective.

TRUFFLES
& treats

PURE DARK CHOCOLATE TRUFFLES

Chocolate "truffles" are so called as they resemble the prized knobbly fungus found under trees. They are supposed to be slightly misshapen, making them the ideal chocolate treat to make at home! A classic truffle is made by creating a ganache, a blend of fresh cream and chocolate, forming a ball and then either rolling it in a finish or dipping it in chocolate to seal. You can make them either way, but be aware that truffles not dipped in chocolate will have to be eaten within a few days of making. My mantra is the same, whether making truffles at Chococo or at home—keep it simple. Use the best ingredients you can find and you will create truffles with a delicious mouthfeel and pure taste.

5 oz. dark chocolate (65–70% cocoa solids, ideally Madagascan or Venezuelan)
3/4 cup whipping cream
1 teaspoon light brown sugar

TO FINISH
6 tablespoons cocoa powder
7 oz. dark chocolate (70% cocoa solids)
1/2 cup of your preferred finish: such as cocoa powder, superfine sugar, sanding sugar, confectioners' sugar, cocoa nibs, desiccated coconut, chopped hazelnuts, chopped pistachio nuts, or edible gold leaf

2–3 baking sheets, lined with baking parchment

a piping bag fitted with a 1-inch nozzle (optional)

Makes 30–35 truffles

TO MAKE THE GANACHE
Chop the chocolate into small pieces and put in a large heatproof bowl.

Put the cream and sugar in a saucepan and heat, stirring gently, until it comes to a rolling boil. Take the pan off the heat and wait for the mixture to stop bubbling before pouring it over the chocolate in the bowl—too hot and it will scorch the chocolate. Stir until it blends into a thick chocolate ganache. Chill the ganache in the fridge for at least 1 hour before using, until thickened.

TO MAKE THE TRUFFLE BALLS
Whisk the chilled ganache with a handheld electric mixer for a few minutes until light and mousse-like. If it is too chilled and has set solid, you will need to whisk for a little longer. Be careful not to overwhisk though as it could start to split (if it does, see Claire's Tip on page 20).

Spoon the whipped ganache into the prepared piping bag and pipe little balls onto the prepared baking sheets.

Alternatively, if you don't have a piping bag, you can make the truffles by hand. Simply put some cocoa powder on your hands and use a teaspoon to scoop a small amount from the whipped ganache, then roll it around in between your hands to make a ball. Put each one on a prepared baking sheet as you work.

Once made, chill the truffle balls on the baking sheets in the fridge for about 15 minutes, until they are firm.

The truffles are now ready to finish as preferred, following the instructions given on the following pages. Before you start, prepare your work trays. You will need a flat surface (a baking sheet or tea tray) for each of your finishes and another parchment paper lined baking tray to put the finished truffles on.

SIMPLE FINISH

If you just want to cover the truffles without dipping them in chocolate first, cover a work tray with your preferred finish. Place each truffle ball on top of the finish and sprinkle your chosen finish over the truffles with a spoon, ensuring they are covered before gently rolling them. Be careful not to dent them as they will be soft. Transfer each truffle to the lined baking sheet as you work.

Store the finished truffles in an airtight container in the fridge and eat within a few days (although as with any food containing fresh cream, they are best eaten as soon as possible).

CHOCOLATE DIPPED

Temper the dark chocolate following the instructions given on page 12. While the chocolate is melting, cover a work tray with your preferred finish.

Using a fork, dip each truffle ball into the melted chocolate. Gently tap the fork on the edge of the bowl to help remove excess chocolate from the truffle.

Carefully put the dipped truffle on the finishing tray and check that it is totally sealed with chocolate—use the fork to cover any holes. Sprinkle your chosen finish over the top of the truffles with a spoon then gently roll them in the finish. Don't be tempted to roll them too

soon as the chocolate will take a few minutes to set firm enough. Transfer the finished truffles to the baking sheet lined with baking parchment as you work.

Alternatively, if you are feeling very confident with your chocolate temper, place the dipped truffles directly on the lined baking sheet and sprinkle your chosen finish over the top of them or add any decoration you are using, such as gold leaf. This is best done with tweezers. Put the tray of finished truffles in a cool place to set.

Store the truffles in an airtight container in the fridge for up to 14 days. (These dipped truffles will keep longer than those with a simple finish.)

CLAIRE'S TIP

What do you do if your ganache "splits"? When blending a ganache, the chocolate and cream can sometimes separate rather than forming a luscious thick chocolate cream. This can happen for various reasons and my advice is not to worry, it is usually fixable. For small quantities of ganache, as in these recipes, let the ganache cool and then bring another $\frac{1}{4}$ cup cream to a boil. Add to the ganache, stirring all the time. Doing so should help "bond" the fats in the chocolate and cream again and restore the ganache to a glossy cream.

HEATHER HONEY TRUFFLES

This is an adaptation of our popular "Bob's Bees" Purbeck honey chocolate, and I suggest that if you can, you use a local heather honey, to make this truffle as personal to your part of the world as "Bob's Bees" is to ours.

3½ oz. dark chocolate (70% cocoa solids and ideally from Ecuador or Grenada), chopped
1¾ oz. semi-sweet chocolate (35–40% cocoa solids), chopped
⅓ cup whipping cream
1 tablespoon honey

TO FINISH
7 oz. dark chocolate (70% cocoa solids), if you want to dip the truffles
sanding sugar or cane sugar

2–3 baking sheets, lined with baking parchment

Makes 20–25 truffles

Chop both the dark and semi-sweet chocolates into small pieces and put in a large heatproof bowl. Set the bowl over a pan of barely simmering water to let the chocolate just soften. Take off the heat when soft but not totally liquid.

Put the cream and honey in a saucepan. Heat gently until it just comes to a boil and stir gently. Take the pan off the heat and wait for the mixture to stop bubbling before pouring it over the softened chocolate in the bowl. Stir the chocolate and cream together until they blend into a thick chocolate ganache.

Chill the ganache in the fridge for at least 1 hour, until firm. Follow the instructions given on pages 18–21 to roll and finish the truffles.

PRUNE & ARMAGNAC TRUFFLES

These are definitely truffles for wintertime, perfect for indulging in during the holiday season, or for including in a gift basket. The flavors are even better if you can marinate the prunes in Armagnac for several weeks beforehand.

½ cup pitted Agen prunes
Armagnac, for soaking and flavoring
5½ oz. dark chocolate (65–70% cocoa solids and ideally from Madagascar), chopped
¾ cup whipping cream
1 teaspoon brown sugar

TO FINISH
7 oz. dark chocolate (70% cocoa solids), if you want to dip the truffles

2–3 baking sheets, lined with baking parchment

Makes 25–30 truffles

Put the prunes in a non-reactive bowl and pour over about 4 tablespoons of Armagnac. Cover and leave to soak for as long as possible (topping up the Armagnac as necessary).

Chop the chocolate into small pieces and put in a large heatproof bowl.

Put the cream and sugar in a saucepan and heat gently until it just comes to a boil. Take the pan off the heat and wait for the mixture to stop bubbling before pouring it over the chopped chocolate in the bowl. Stir the chocolate and cream together until they blend into a thick chocolate ganache.

Purée the marinated prunes in a blender and add to the ganache, along with 1–2 teaspoons of the soaking juice, or more Armagnac to taste, as preferred. Stir to mix in.

Chill the ganache in the fridge for at least 1 hour, until firm. Follow the instructions given on pages 18–21 to roll and finish the truffles.

SPRING SAFFRON TRUFFLES

This precious aromatic spice is more usually associated with savory dishes but is equally delicious when blended with fine chocolate. Keeping it simple allows the flavors to shine through and this is a sophisticated treat for fans of saffron.

5½ oz. semi-sweet chocolate (35–40% cocoa solids and ideally from Venezuela), chopped
a generous pinch of saffron strands (about 30–35)
⅓ cup whipping cream

TO FINISH
7 oz. dark chocolate (70% cocoa solids) sanding sugar or edible gold leaf

2–3 baking sheets, lined with baking parchment

Makes 20–25 truffles

Chop the chocolate into small pieces and put in a large heatproof bowl set over a saucepan of barely simmering water. Take off the heat when softened but not completely melted.

Put the saffron in a mortar and add 1 teaspoon warm water. Let steep for a few minutes then bash with the pestle to soften the strands.

Put the cream in a saucepan, add the saffron and warm gently until it just comes to a boil.

Take the pan off the heat and wait for mixture to stop bubbling before pouring it over the softened chocolate in the bowl. Stir the chocolate and cream together until they blend into a thick chocolate ganache.

Chill the ganache in the fridge for at least 1 hour, until firm. Follow the instructions given on pages 18–21 to roll, finish, and decorate the truffles.

FRESH GARDEN MINT TRUFFLES

This is inspired by our award-winning "Mellow Mint" chocolate. You can infuse chocolate with any fresh herbs that you have growing in your garden, but this combination of flavors is my favorite.

3½ oz. dark chocolate (65–70% cocoa solids and ideally from Ecuador or Venezuela), chopped
scant ¾ cup whipping cream
a large handful of fresh mint leaves

TO FINISH
7 oz. dark chocolate (70% cocoa solids), if you want to dip the truffles crystalized mint leaves*

2–3 baking sheets, lined with baking parchment

Makes 20–25 truffles

Chop the chocolate into small pieces and put in a large heatproof bowl.

Put the cream and mint in a saucepan and heat gently until it just comes to a boil. Take the pan off the heat and set aside for 10 minutes, to allow the mint to infuse the cream.

Return the infused cream to the heat and bring back to a boil. Take the pan off the heat, wait for the mixture to stop bubbling and pour it through a strainer onto the chopped chocolate in the bowl. Stir the chocolate and cream together until blended into a thick ganache.

Chill the ganache in the fridge for at least 1 hour, until firm. Follow the instructions given on pages 18–21 to roll, finish, and decorate the truffles.

* **To crystalize mint leaves:** Select the smallest mint leaves from your bunch. Rub each leaf gently with a finger dipped in egg white and sprinkle with superfine sugar. Put on a sheet of baking parchment and leave to set. Use to decorate each truffle.

MAGIC MENDIANTS

These mendiants, or disks, of studded chocolate are simple enough for children to make and are perfect with coffee at the end of a meal or to give as gifts. However, this is also a recipe which ideally requires you to temper the chocolate to reduce the risk of it "blooming" when it sets. The trick here, if you are at all concerned, is to ensure that you cover these disks with their delicious toppings so that it doesn't matter too much! You can vary the toppings to suit your taste but I think this combination tastes particularly fabulous.

14 oz. dark chocolate (70% cocoa solids) or semi-sweet chocolate (35–40% cocoa solids), chopped

2 teaspoons apple pie spice

¾ cup pecans or walnuts

½ cup dried cranberries

½ cup chopped candied orange peel

2–3 baking sheets, lined with baking parchment

Makes about 20 disks

Seed temper the chocolate following the instructions given on page 14.

Add the apple pie spice to the chocolate and stir in. (You will need to work fast here as the chocolate will cool quickly.)

Make rounds on one of the prepared baking sheets by placing a dessertspoon of chocolate onto the sheet and tapping the chocolate off the spoon into disks.

Top the rounds with the nuts, fruits, and candied peel. Gently press down with the back of a spoon to ensure that the topping is embedded in the chocolate.

Repeat until you have used all the chocolate and toppings.

Put the baking sheets in the fridge and chill until set. The mendiants can be stored in an airtight container in a cool place for up to 2 weeks.

DELICIOUS DIPPED FRUITS

Dipping juicy fruits in dark chocolate is not only easy to do, but a relatively healthy sweet treat and also dairy-free. This couldn't be simpler. Choose the fruits you wish to eat, temper some chocolate, dip, and go!

7 oz. dark chocolate (70% cocoa solids), chopped
about 30 bite-size pieces of fresh fruit, such as strawberries, cherries, kiwi, apricots, peaches, and physalis (cape gooseberries)

1–2 baking sheets lined with baking parchment

Serves 4–6

Wash and prepare the fruit as necessary. If using strawberries, cherries and/or physalis, do leave the stalks and hulls on. Pat well with paper towels to remove any excess water.

Temper the chocolate following the instructions given on page 12.

Carefully dip each piece of fruit halfway into the chocolate, tap it on the side of the bowl to remove any excess chocolate, and put on the prepared baking sheets.

Transfer the sheets to a cool place and leave the chocolate to set.

These fruits should be eaten on the day they are made and stored in the fridge until you are ready to serve.

VARIATION

For Dipped Dried Fruits choose a good selection of 24–30 naturally sun-dried fruits, such as: apricots, dates, pineapple, pear, chewy banana chips, mangoes, figs, and prunes.

Follow the instructions for dipping fresh fruits. These will keep stored in an airtight container in a cool place for up to 1 month.

NUTS ABOUT NUTS PRALINE BRITTLE SLABS

Praline is a classic combination, traditionally of crushed hazelnuts, sugar, and chocolate. This is a little twist on that idea creating a slightly crunchier version within a slab of pure chocolate and using pecans, which I think lend themselves beautifully to all things chocolate, but feel free to use whichever nuts you prefer.

½ cup shelled pecans, roughly chopped
½ cup shelled hazelnuts, roughly chopped
1 cup granulated sugar
7 oz. semi–sweet chocolate (minimum 35% cocoa solids), chopped

2 baking sheets, 1 greased with a flavorless oil (such as grapeseed), 1 lined with baking parchment

an oiled metal spatula

Makes about 12 slabs

Put the pecans and hazelnuts in a dry skillet and toast over low heat, shaking the pan constantly to prevent them catching and burning.

Meanwhile, warm a heavy-based saucepan and gradually add the sugar. Try to avoid stirring the sugar, but swirl the pan to spread the sugar around as it melts. Watch it closely as it will burn if you take your eyes off it.

Add the warm toasted nuts to the caramelized sugar and mix well to coat.

Transfer the mixture to the greased baking sheet, taking care as it will be very hot. Spread it out using an oiled metal spatula and level the surface. You will need to work quickly as the mixture will begin to set the moment it leaves the warm saucepan.

Let the praline brittle cool and then chop it into small pieces—you can use a blender to crush into smaller pieces if you prefer a finer finish.

Temper the chocolate following the instructions given on page 12.

Add the chopped praline brittle to the tempered chocolate, mix together to ensure it is well coated, and then pour onto the lined baking sheet.

Let cool and then break into chunks. Eat on its own or serve with vanilla ice cream and a hot sauce (see page 141 for recipes).

The brittle slabs can be stored in an airtight container in a cool place for up to 1 week.

BRITTLE BUZZ BITES

We first created a hemp buzz bar a few years ago at Chococo, (I think we were rather ahead of our time), but this takes the idea further by sealing the freshly toasted taste of the crunchy seeds in a simple caramel and then coating them in chocolate.

⅔ cup shelled hemp seeds

1 cup granulated sugar

7 oz. semi-sweet chocolate (35–40% cocoa solids) or dark chocolate (70% cocoa solids), chopped

2 baking sheets, 1 greased with a flavorless oil (such as grapeseed), 1 lined with baking parchment

an oiled metal spatula

Makes about 40 bites

Put the hemp seeds in a dry skillet and toast over low heat, shaking the pan constantly to prevent them catching and burning.

Meanwhile, warm a heavy-based saucepan and gradually add the sugar. Try to avoid stirring the sugar, but swirl the pan to spread the sugar around as it melts. Watch it closely as it will burn if you take your eyes off it.

Add the warm toasted seeds to the caramelized sugar and mix well to coat.

Transfer the mixture to the greased baking sheet, taking care as it will be very hot.

Spread it out using an oiled metal spatula and level the surface. You will need to work quickly as the mixture will begin to set the moment it leaves the warm saucepan. Allow the brittle to cool at room temperature and then break it up into bite-size chunks.

While the brittle is cooling, seed temper the chocolate following the instructions given on page 14.

Dip each of the brittle chunks into the tempered chocolate, using 2 forks to fish each chunk out again and put on the lined baking sheet.

Let cool and eat on its own or serve with vanilla ice cream.

The brittle bites can be stored in an airtight container in a cool place for up to 1 week.

VARIATION

Replace the hemp seeds with ½ cup sesame seeds or ⅔ cup pine nuts and make in exactly the same way. Both options are just as delicious!

STUDDED SLABS

Making slabs studded with "goodies", as my dad would say, is a great way to use up any chocolate left over from making other treats such as truffles. Here are three recipes to get your creative juices flowing.

AZTEC SPICE

If you like your chocolate dark and spicy, this is for you! This also makes a great gift for a man.

7 oz. dark chocolate (70% cocoa solids), chopped

1–2 teaspoons dried hot pepper flakes, to taste

½ tablespoon roasted

cocoa nibs

4 grinds of black pepper

a jelly roll pan or baking sheet with sides, lined with baking parchment

Temper the chocolate following the instructions given on page 12. Pour the tempered chocolate into the prepared pan. Sprinkle the hot pepper flakes, cocoa nibs, and black pepper over the melted chocolate.

Leave to cool, ideally in a cool, dry place, but if the only cool option is the fridge, be aware that it might bloom with the temperature change, but this won't affect the flavor. Once set, break into shards and store in an airtight container in a cool place for up to 2 weeks.

TROPICAL TRAIL

This is a sweeter option for tropical fruit fans and another crafty way of encouraging little people to eat fruit.

a handful of fresh coconut slices

7 oz. semi-sweet chocolate (40% cocoa solids), chopped

¼ cup sweetened dried papaya pieces

¼ cup banana chips

¼ cup sweetened dried pineapple pieces

a jelly roll pan or baking sheet with sides, lined with baking parchment

Tear the coconut into smaller pieces and toast in a dry skillet until lightly browned.

Temper the chocolate following the instructions given on page 12. Pour the tempered chocolate into the prepared pan. Sprinkle the coconut and other ingredients over the melted chocolate.

Leave to cool, ideally in a cool, dry place, but if the only cool option is the fridge, be aware that it might bloom with the temperature change, but won't affect the flavor. Once set, break into shards and store in an airtight container in a cool place for up to 2 weeks.

EXOTIC SPICE

A combination of delicious crystalized ginger and toasted sesame seeds.

7 oz. dark chocolate (70% cocoa solids), chopped

¼ cup chopped crystalized ginger

1 teaspoon sesame seeds

a jelly roll pan or baking sheet with sides, lined with baking parchment

Toast the sesame seeds in a dry skillet until lightly browned and fragrant.

Temper the chocolate following the instructions given on page 12. Pour the tempered chocolate into the prepared pan. Sprinkle the sesame seeds and ginger over the melted chocolate.

Leave to cool, ideally in a cool, dry place, but if the only cool option is the fridge, be aware that it might bloom with the temperature change, but this won't affect the flavor. Once set, break into shards and store in an airtight container in a cool place for up to 2 weeks.

FABULOUSLY FRUITY SALAMI

This delicious and fun chocolate delight takes its inspiration from Italian chocolate salamis traditionally sold at Christmas. This is definitely a holiday treat to add to your list, but I also think it works at any time of year and makes a stunning finish to a dinner, served with a glass of chilled dessert wine. I love the combination of rich dried fruits with a hint of orange in the chocolate, but you can always vary the fruits and nuts to suit your own taste. Just keep the quantities the same and ensure that you chop the ingredients up small so that the finished "salami" can be easily sliced by your guests.

5 oz. dark chocolate (70% cocoa solids), chopped
3 tablespoons unsalted butter, chilled and cut into pieces
3/4 cup dried figs (ideally soft partially rehydrated ones)
1/2 cup pitted dates
1/3 cup dried apricots (ideally sundried for their intense flavor)
1/3 cup raisins, chopped
1/3 cup almonds, very finely chopped
3 tablespoons candied orange peel, chopped
3 tablespoons sifted confectioners' sugar

a baking sheet, lined with 2 layers of plastic wrap

Serves 10–12

Put the chocolate and butter in a heatproof bowl and set over a saucepan of gently simmering water. Do not allow the base of the bowl to touch the water.

While the chocolate is melting, chop the fruits and nuts into the smallest pieces you can. Once the chocolate has melted, take it off the heat and stir in the chopped fruits and nuts.

Leave the mixture to cool for about 10 minutes then pour the cooled mixture onto the prepared baking sheet.

Bring up the sides of the plastic wrap and fold it over the chocolate mixture to form a long salami shape, about 12 inches long. Roll the warm mixture around on the baking sheet to form a salami shape.

Put the salami in the fridge (still on the baking sheet) and if you can, take it out of the fridge every 10–15 minutes to roll it on a flat surface. This helps ensure that it sets in a cylindrical shape and not with a flat bottom. It will take at least 2 hours to set firm so be patient and don't try to make this at the last minute!

About 10 minutes before you want to serve the salami, take it out of the fridge and let it return to room temperature before removing the plastic wrap.

Just before serving, roll the salami in the confectioners' sugar on a clean work surface and trim the ends to show the wonderful speckled interior.

Either cut into slices or serve the salami whole with a knife for others to cut their own slices to suit.

The salami will keep in the fridge for 1 week and if, when taking it out of the fridge, the confectioners' sugar melts away, just re-roll it in more sugar to refresh the finish.

ROCKY ROAD SAUSAGE

This is a child-friendly "salami", which my two kids, Lily and Max, love making, and has a rather useful added benefit for a parent in that you can control the quantities devoured each time, more so than if you make the more usual rocky road cakes or bars.

My recipe also has dark chocolate in it to cut through the sweetness of semi-sweet chocolate and includes more interesting dried fruits than you might find in other similar recipes.

5 oz. dark chocolate
   (70% cocoa solids),
   chopped
4 oz. semi-sweet
   chocolate (minimum
   35% cocoa solids),
   chopped
4 oz. graham crackers
   or digestive biscuits
2/3 cups mixed dried
   fruits, such as
   blueberries, raisins,
   sour cherries, and
   cranberries,
   finely chopped
1 cup mini marshmallows
3 tablespoons sifted
   confectioners' sugar

a baking sheet, lined with
2 layers of plastic wrap

Serves 8–10

Put the chocolates in a heatproof bowl and set over a saucepan of gently simmering water. Do not allow the base of the bowl to touch the water.

While the chocolates are melting, break up the crackers by hand or put them in a polythene bag and bash with a rolling pin. Don't crush them to a powder, you need chunks not crumbs.

Once the chocolate has melted, take it off the heat and add the broken crackers, chopped fruits, and marshmallows to the bowl. Stir well to mix.

Leave the mixture to cool for about 10 minutes then transfer to the prepared baking sheet.

Bring up the sides of the plastic wrap and fold it over the chocolate mixture to form a long sausage shape, about 12 inches long. Roll the warm mixture around on the baking sheet to form a sausage shape.

Put the sausage in the fridge (still on the baking sheet) and if you can, take it out of the fridge every 10–15 minutes to roll it on a flat surface. This helps ensure that it sets in a cylindrical shape and not with a flat bottom. It will take at least 2 hours to set firm so be patient and don't try to make this at the last minute!

About 10 minutes before you want to serve the sausage, take it out of the fridge and let it return to room temperature before removing the plastic wrap.

Just before serving, roll the sausage in the confectioners' sugar on a clean work surface. Cut into slices to serve.

This will keep in the fridge for 1 week and if, when taking it out of the fridge, the confectioners' sugar melts away, just re-roll it in more sugar to refresh the finish.

CARDAMOM, PISTACHIO, & CHEESE PARCELS

This recipe is a guaranteed conversation starter and brilliant for a party as an interestingly alternative sweet nibble.

Each phyllo parcel blends cardamom and pistachio, the flavors in a "Green Spice" truffle, one of our more idiosyncratic chocolates, along with creamy cheeses and a little white chocolate for sweetness.

3 cardamom pods
½ cup ricotta
2 tablespoons soft goat cheese
¼ cup cream cheese
½ cup shelled pistachio nuts, finely chopped
2 oz. white chocolate, finely chopped
25 rectangles of phyllo dough (each about 5 x 3 inches)
2 tablespoons unsalted butter, melted
sifted confectioners' sugar, to dust

a baking sheet, lined with baking parchment

Makes 25 parcels

Preheat the oven to 375°F.

Break open the cardamom pods, scoop out the seeds, and crush them to a powder in a mortar with a pestle.

Put the cheeses in a bowl and beat together with a wooden spoon. Add the pistachios, crushed cardamom seeds, and chocolate.

Put a phyllo rectangle on a clean work surface so that the short edge is in front of you and the length going away from you. Brush it with some melted butter.

Place a teaspoonful of filling 1½ inches from the end closest to you and slightly to the left of center. (Do not be tempted to put too much in each parcel as the filling will spread and if you overfill them it might escape.) Fold the phyllo edge nearest you over the filling and seal it in

on all sides. Then take the new bottom left corner and rotate the parcel up the right-hand side of the rectangle to form a triangle. Repeat the process by taking the new bottom right and rolling the triangle up the right-hand side of the rectangle. Then for the last roll, rotate the triangle over to the top left and with the remaining pastry, fold it over to seal the edge, using a little more melted butter if necessary to ensure it is sealed.

Put the parcel on the prepared baking sheet and repeat the process until all the phyllo and filling has been used. Brush each parcel with the remaining butter and bake in the preheated oven for about 12–15 minutes, until golden brown.

Dust liberally with sifted confectioners' sugar and serve warm. These parcels are best eaten on the day they are made.

DINKY VANILLA CHOCOLATE TARTS

The Australian chef Bill Grainger is one of my food heroes and this recipe is my adaptation of his custard tarts. These chocolate tarts with a vanilla-infused set custard-style filling make lovely party nibbles or a light dessert, but I warn you now, that one will just not be enough! I like to serve these just warmed through and lightly dusted with sugar. Do cook them in batches if you have only one suitable pan. It's fine to use prepared puff pastry dough but do look for brands labeled "all-butter" as these will be superior in quality and taste.

3 egg yolks

¼ cup granulated sugar

2 tablespoons cornstarch, sifted

1 teaspoon vanilla extract

1 cup heavy cream

1 vanilla bean

5½ oz. dark chocolate (70% cocoa solids), chopped

sifted confectioners' sugar, to dust

13-oz. sheet prepared frozen puff pastry dough, defrosted

two or three 12-cup mini muffin pans, lightly greased with butter

Makes about 30 tarts

Preheat the oven to 400°F.

Put the egg yolks, sugar, cornstarch, and vanilla extract in a bowl and mix together with a balloon whisk until smooth. Add the cream and generous ⅓ cup cold water to the mixture and whisk together.

Split the vanilla bean using a sharp knife and use the tip to scrape the seeds directly into the custard mixture. Add the bean to the bowl too.

Pour the mixture into a saucepan and set over medium heat. Cook for 4–5 minutes, until the mixture starts to thicken, stirring continuously to prevent any lumps forming.

The minute it reaches a boil, take the custard off the heat, remove the vanilla bean, and then add the chopped chocolate, stirring continuously as it melts. Set aside to cool. (You can make the custard filling ahead of time as it will keep overnight in the fridge.)

To prepare the pastry cases, unroll the puff pastry dough on a floured work surface and re-roll it up tightly starting at the short side. Cut narrow rings of just ¼ inch and roll each one out to a thin circle of no more than 3 inches diameter.

Line each cup in the prepared muffin pans with a pastry round, overlapping any excess pastry around the rim as you go, which gives the distinctive custard tart look when they cook.

Put the pans in the fridge for a few minutes to chill the pastry before filling each tart case with 2 teaspoonfuls of the chocolate custard mixture.

Bake in the preheated oven for about 15 minutes, until the pastry is golden brown and the custard has puffed up in the middle. (The custard will sink as the tarts cool, so don't be alarmed when that happens.)

Let the tarts cool in the pans before removing. Serve warm and dusted with sifted confectioners' sugar.

CAKES
& bakes

DARK & LIGHT CHOCOLATE CHILI CAKE

This deliciously light flourless cake with a hint of spicy chili, takes its inspiration from the importance of corn (the light) and cacao (the dark) to the Mayans and Aztecs of Central America, for whom both foods were central to their complex cultures. Cacao and corn were combined in beverages for religious rituals and offered to the gods to help ensure healthy crops. These drinks also included ingredients such as chili, honey, and vanilla, so this cake pays homage to the people who first cultivated cocoa!

7 oz. dark chocolate (70% cocoa solids) chopped
1 stick plus 2 tablespoons unsalted butter, chilled and cut into pieces
1 tablespoon clear honey
5 eggs, separated
2 teaspoons vanilla extract
⅓ cup packed light brown sugar
⅓ cup instant polenta or fine-ground cornmeal
1 teaspoon baking powder
¼ teaspoon crushed sea salt
1 teaspoon chili powder*

TO DECORATE
sifted confectioners' sugar, to dust
sifted cocoa powder, to dust

a 9-inch loose-based cake pan, greased and lined with baking parchment

Serves 8

Preheat the oven to 350°F.

Put the chocolate, butter, and honey in a saucepan. Melt over low heat and set aside to cool.

Cream the egg yolks, vanilla extract, and sugar together in a large bowl until creamy and light in color.

In a clean, grease-free bowl whisk the egg whites with a handheld electric mixer, until stiffly peaking.

Gently mix the cooled chocolate mixture into the egg yolk mixture and then add the polenta, baking powder, sea salt, and chili powder.

Gradually fold the egg whites into the mixture using a metal spoon—as gently as you can so that you don't lose the air in the eggs.

Bake in the preheated oven for about 25–30 minutes, until the cake has risen and a skewer inserted in the center comes out clean. The cake will sink as it cools so don't worry when that happens.

Once cool, I like to give this cake a very simple "dark and light" decoration of a dark cocoa powder heart on top of confectioners' sugar (which is very symbolic as Mesoamerican rituals sometimes involved removing the hearts of human sacrifices and mixing the blood with cacao to drink... they were quite a blood-thirsty lot!). This amuses me but you can create any pattern you like.

To make a heart stencil, draw around the cake pan on baking parchment, cut out the circle, fold it in half, and cut out a half heart shape to create a symmetrical heart when unfolded.

Liberally dust the entire cake in sifted confectioners' sugar. Put the stencil on top and dust through the cut-out heart with sifted cocoa powder to finish.

The cake will keep stored in an airtight container for 1–2 days.

* **Note:** We use Mexican ancho chili powder at Chococo as it has a mild, well-rounded flavor that works well with chocolate. Look out for it in the specialist sections of good supermarkets, online spice suppliers, or in delicatessens, but if you cannot find it, use a good-quality mild chili powder instead.

DEVILISHLY DELICIOUS CHOCOLATE CAKE

This is my version of the birthday cake of choice for both my sister Frances and myself as teenagers. A family favorite and, I gather, a turn-of-the-20th-century American creation. Yes, it's rich, but oh so lovely for any celebration!

scant 1 cup whole milk
1 tablespoon freshly
    squeezed lemon juice
1½ cups all-purpose flour
1 teaspoon baking soda
½ cup cocoa powder
6½ tablespoons unsalted
    butter, softened
1 cup plus 2 tablespoons
    granulated sugar
3 eggs, lightly beaten
white and dark chocolate
    curls, to decorate
    (see page 15)

FROSTING
7 oz. dark chocolate
    (70% cocoa solids),
    chopped
1 cup mascarpone
1–2 tablespoons sifted
    confectioners' sugar

*two 8-inch diameter cake
pans, greased*

Serves 8

Preheat the oven to 350°F.

Pour the milk into a pitcher, add the lemon juice and leave to sour while you prepare the rest of the ingredients.

Sift the flour, baking soda, and cocoa powder together into a bowl.

Cream the butter and sugar together in a large bowl until creamy and light in color. Gradually add the eggs to the sugar and butter mixture.

Alternately fold the sour milk and flour into the egg mixture, until everything is mixed together.

Divide the mixture between the prepared baking pans and tap them to ensure they are level.

Bake in the preheated oven for about 25 minutes, until a skewer inserted in the center comes out clean and a cake bounces back when lightly pressed.

Leave the cakes to cool in the pans for about 10 minutes before turning out onto a wire rack to cool. While the cakes are cooling, make the frosting.

Melt the chocolate in a heatproof bowl set over a saucepan of gently simmering water. Take the bowl off the pan and leave to cool for 5 minutes.

Add the mascarpone and confectioners' sugar to taste. (I add only 1 tablespoon as I like a relatively sharp frosting but if you want a sweeter one, add a second tablespoon.) Beat until light and fluffy, ideally using a handheld electric mixer.

Working quickly, as the frosting will quickly start to set, sandwich the cakes together with half of the frosting and cover the cake with the remainder.

Decoration is entirely up to you. Choose from white and milk chocolate curls, sprinkles, traditional sweets, candles, or even sparklers.

The cake will keep stored in an airtight container in the fridge for up to 2 days.

TRIPLE CHOCOLATE CUPSIDE-DOWN CAKES

These are really chocolatey mini cakes drizzled with fresh cream chocolate ganache, rather than classic American-style cupcakes piled high with a sweet, whipped frosting. I like decorating half a batch with a white chocolate ganache and the other half with dark, as not only will you appeal to more people, they also look lovely when arranged together.

If you are taking your cakes out and about, it may be better to decorate them in their paper cases the right way up, but the team here at Chococo all think that they are much nicer upside down as you get to enjoy more of the ganache…

- 1 stick plus 6 tablespoons unsalted butter, at room temperature
- ¾ cup packed light brown sugar
- 3 eggs (see Claire's Tip)
- 2½ oz. semi-sweet chocolate (minimum 35% cocoa solids), chopped
- 2½ oz. white chocolate, chopped into chunks
- 1 teaspoon vanilla extract
- 1¼ cups self-rising flour
- ¼ cup cocoa powder
- ¼ teaspoon baking powder

**SIMPLE WHITE
CHOCOLATE GANACHE**
3½ oz. white chocolate,
  chopped
⅓ cup crème fraîche or
  sour cream

**SIMPLE DARK
CHOCOLATE GANACHE**
2½ oz. dark chocolate,
  chopped
½ scant cup heavy cream
1 teaspoon confectioners'
  sugar (optional)

TO DECORATE
fresh raspberries
natural glacé cherries
white and milk chocolate
  curls (see page 15)
dragees or sprinkles

*a 12-cup cupcake or
muffin pan, lined with
paper cases*

Makes 12 cakes

Preheat the oven to 350°F.

Cream the butter and sugar together
in a large bowl with a handheld electric
mixer, until creamy and light in color.
Gradually add the eggs to the sugar and
butter mixture. Then add the chopped
milk and white chocolates and vanilla
extract and stir in with a wooden spoon.

Sift in the flour, cocoa powder, and
baking powder and fold in using a
tablespoon. (Do not overwork the cake
batter as it will make your cakes heavy.)

Spoon the batter into the paper cases,
leaving a little space at the top for the
cakes to rise.

Bake in the preheated oven for about
20 minutes, until a skewer inserted in
the center comes out clean and a cake
bounces back when lightly pressed.
Leave to cool in the pan for a few
minutes before transferring to a wire
rack to cool completely.

Make up the ganaches as required.
(Simply double the quantities if you
are making just one type.) Put the
chocolate, crème fraîche or cream,
and confectioners' sugar (if using, it's
optional for a dark ganache) in a small
heavy-based saucepan set over low heat.
Stir gently until the chocolate melts into
the cream.

Take off the heat and leave for a few
minutes to cool and thicken slightly
before using.

Peel the paper cases off the cakes and
turn them upside down on the wire rack.
(Slide a piece of baking parchment
underneath to catch any drips.) Pour
a little of the ganache onto what is
now the top of each cake and allow
it to drizzle down the sides.

Decoration is entirely up to you; choose
from fresh raspberries, natural glacé
cherries, white and dark chocolate curls,
dragees, or sprinkles. Put your chosen
decoration on the top of the cakes at
this stage as the ganache cools and sets.
(If your ganache has thickened too much,
add a little warm cream to loosen it.)

The cupcakes will keep stored in an
airtight container in the fridge for
up to 2 days.

CLAIRE'S TIP
For best results when baking any sponge
cake, weigh your eggs before you start.
They should weigh the same in their
shells as the individual quantities of
butter and flour. If not, adjust both the
butter and flour quantities accordingly.

CHOCOCO SURPRISE CAKE

This fun cake breaks all my rules about not using food colorings when baking but our kids just love making it. Outwardly it looks like a classic sponge cake with ganache and chocolate curls, but when cut open, reveals its colorful surprise. Its "wow" factor makes it a great cake for birthday parties.

2 sticks unsalted butter,
  at room temperature
2¼ cups granulated sugar
1 teaspoon vanilla extract
4 eggs, lightly beaten
  (see Claire's Tip
  page 51)
2 cups self-rising flour
¼ teaspoon baking
  powder
1 tablespoon whole milk,
  if required
red and green food
  coloring (or other
  colors of your choice)

CHOCOLATE GANACHE
7 oz. dark chocolate,
  chopped
1 cup heavy cream
2 tablespoons softened
  unsalted butter

TO DECORATE
3½ oz. semi-sweet
  chocolate curls
  (see page 15)
sifted confectioners'
  sugar, to dust
sprinkles and/or edible
  silver balls (optional)

*two 8-inch diameter cake
pans, greased*

Serves 8–10

Preheat the oven to 350°F.

Cream the butter and sugar together in a large bowl with a handheld electric mixer, until creamy and light in color. Add the vanilla extract and gradually beat in the eggs a little at a time. Sift in the flour and baking powder and fold in gently with a tablespoon. If the mixture feels very stiff, add the milk to loosen it.

Divide the mixture between 3 separate bowls. Add a touch of food coloring to 2 of the bowls, leaving one untinted. I like to add just a little coloring (about ¼ teaspoon) to make my cake pastel colors, but do add more if you want them more vibrant. Stir in the colorings gently—you do not want to overwork the cake batter at this point as it will make your cake heavy.

Put small dollops of the 3 mixtures in the prepared pans in a random pattern and then level the top with a palette knife.

Bake in the preheated oven for about 20–25 minutes, until a skewer inserted in the center comes out clean and a cake bounces back when lightly pressed.

Leave the cakes to cool in the pan for a few minutes before turning out onto a wire rack to cool completely.

To make the ganache, put the chocolate, cream and butter in a heavy-based saucepan and set over low heat. Stir gently until the chocolate melts into the cream. Take off the heat and leave for a few minutes to cool and thicken slightly before using.

Spread about 5 heaping tablespoons of the ganache over one half of the cooled cake and sandwich together with the other half. This is best done while the cake is still on the wire rack and with a sheet of baking parchment underneath to catch any drips. Working quickly, pour the rest of the ganache over the top of the cake and smooth it over the top and sides with a palette knife.

To finish, I like to arrange chocolate curls in the center of the cake and simply dust with a little confectioners' sugar or add some sprinkles, but you can decorate it however you choose.

The cake will keep stored in an airtight container in the fridge for up to 2 days.

LEMON ZING ROULADE

Although this looks like a rich sponge cake it is flourless and surprisingly light. The recipe is inspired by our "Lemon Zing" chocolate, which is filled with fresh lemon curd, handmade locally for us. You can of course buy good quality lemon curd, but if you have the time, I would recommend that you make your own, as trust me, you will notice the difference. The secret with a roulade is keeping it as moist as you can before rolling it. It will crack as you roll it, but don't worry, it's all part of its charm.

ROULADE
5½ oz. dark chocolate, chopped
4 eggs, separated
½ cup granulated sugar
1 teaspoon vanilla extract

FILLING
1 cup mascarpone
2 tablespoons confectioners' sugar
1 scant cup (8 oz.) lemon curd
finely grated peel of ½ a lemon

TO DECORATE
2 oz. dark chocolate curls (see page 15)
sifted cocoa powder, to dust
sifted confectioners' sugar, to dust
grated peel of ½ a lemon

a 9 x 13 inch jelly roll pan, greased and lined with baking parchment

2 clean kitchen towels

a large baking sheet

Serves 8–10

Preheat the oven to 350°F.

To make the roulade, put the chocolate in a heatproof bowl set over a saucepan of barely simmering water. Do not let the base of the bowl touch the water. Take the bowl off the pan once melted and let cool for a few minutes.

Beat together the egg yolks, sugar, and vanilla extract in a large bowl until creamy and thick, and then stir in the cooled melted chocolate.

Whisk the egg whites in a separate grease-free bowl with a handheld electric mixer until stiffly peaking. Gradually fold the egg whites into the egg and sugar mixture using a rubber spatula.

Pour the mixture into the prepared pan and level the surface. Bake in the preheated oven for 15–20 minutes, until risen and firm but don't overcook it as you don't want the roulade to be dry.

Place a clean kitchen towel over the cooked roulade. Rinse a second kitchen towel in hot water and wring it out. Put it on top of the first kitchen towel. Leave the covered roulade in its pan until cold.

When the roulade is cold, sift cocoa powder and confectioners' sugar over a large piece of baking parchment, turn the roulade out onto this paper and peel away the original lining paper.

To make the filling, whip the mascarpone and confectioners' sugar together then mix in the lemon curd and grated peel.

Trim off the edges from the roulade then spread your filling over it, leaving about ½ inch around each edge. To roll up the roulade, start at the short end nearest to you and roll it away from you, using the baking parchment underneath it to help you form the roll.

Dust the roulade liberally with more confectioners' sugar and finish with the chocolate curls and grated lemon peel. Use a fish slice to transfer it to a serving plate and cut into slices with a hot serrated knife to serve.

The roulade is best eaten on the day it is made but will keep stored in an airtight container in the fridge for up to 2 days.

BRILLIANT BLUEBERRY MUFFINS WITH LEMON & WHITE CHOCOLATE

We are very lucky to have a local blueberry farm here in Purbeck and this muffin is a celebration of these fabulous fruits, married here with tangy lemon and creamy white chocolate. I think these muffins are at their most delicious when made with English blueberries in season, but you can still bake them at any time of year using fresh or frozen fruit.

1 stick plus 4 tablespoons
  unsalted butter
²/₃ cup whole milk
2²/₃ cups self-rising flour
³/₄ cup granulated sugar
1 teaspoon baking
  powder
2 tablespoons freshly
  squeezed lemon juice
2 eggs, beaten
finely grated peel of
  1 lemon
1 teaspoon vanilla extract
3½ oz. white chocolate,
  roughly chopped
1 cup blueberries
raw sugar, to sprinkle

*a 12-cup muffin pan, lined
with paper cases*

Makes 12 muffins

Preheat the oven to 350°F.

Put the butter and milk in a saucepan and heat gently until the butter melts. Take off the heat and leave to cool for 5 minutes.

Put the flour, sugar, and baking powder into a large bowl and make a well in the center.

Add the lemon juice to the milk and butter mixture and then add the wet mixture to the dry ingredients and stir together. Don't overmix the batter as this will make the muffins tough.

Stir in the eggs, then add the grated lemon peel, vanilla, chocolate, and ²/₃ cup of the blueberries, reserving the remainder to top the muffins.

Fill each muffin case two-thirds of the way up (to give them room to rise) and then squash 2–3 extra blueberries into the top of each muffin and sprinkle with a little raw sugar.

Bake in the preheated oven for about 20–25 minutes, until risen, golden brown on top and a skewer inserted in the center of a muffin comes out clean.

Allow the muffins to cool in the pan for a few minutes before transferring them to a wire rack to cool completely.

The muffins will keep stored in an airtight container for 3–4 days, but do warm them before eating.

CHEEKY MONKEY MUFFINS WITH DARK CHOCOLATE & BANANA

Banana and chocolate is a favorite flavor combination with kids of all ages and works brilliantly in this moist muffin, which is packed full of not just bananas but also dates, orange-infused golden raisins, a hint of cinnamon, and plenty of chunks of dark chocolate to keep the chocaholics happy. A popular choice in our café, these muffins are perfect for all the cheeky monkeys about to embark on adventures requiring an energy fix! They are at their most delicious served warm, and can be frozen for up to 2 weeks if you are super organized. To serve, simply let defrost and warm in a low oven.

¾ cup golden raisins
⅓ cup freshly squeezed
    orange juice
2 cups all-purpose flour
1 teaspoon baking soda
1 teaspoon baking
    powder
¾ cup chopped dates
3 oz. dark chocolate,
    chopped
1 teaspoon ground
    cinnamon
1 egg, beaten
⅓ cup granulated sugar
5 tablespoons unsalted
    butter, melted
2 large or 3 small
    bananas, mashed
¾ cup whole milk
raw sugar, to sprinkle

*a 12-cup muffin pan,
lined with paper cases*

Makes 12 muffins

Preheat the oven to 350°F.

Put the golden raisins in a small saucepan and add the orange juice. Bring to a boil then take off the heat and set aside to allow the raisins to plump up.

Put the flour, baking soda, baking powder, ½ cup of the dates, the chocolate, and cinnamon in a separate bowl and make a well in the center.

Beat the egg and sugar together, then add the melted butter, bananas, milk, and orange juice-soaked raisins.

Add the egg mixture to the dry ingredients and stir together.

Don't overmix the batter as this will make the muffins tough. The batter will be quite runny but that's nothing to worry about.

Fill each muffin case two-thirds of the way up (to give them room to rise). Scatter the remaining chopped dates on top of each muffin and sprinkle with the raw sugar.

Bake in the preheated oven for about 20–25 minutes, until golden brown and a skewer inserted in the center of a muffin comes out clean.

Allow the muffins to cool in the pan for a few minutes before transferring to a wire rack to cool completely.

The muffins will keep stored in an airtight container for 3–4 days, or can be frozen for up to 2 weeks. Do warm them in a low oven before eating.

SCRUMPTIOUS SALTED CARAMEL SHORTBREAD

This is my 21st-century twist on a classic afternoon tea treat which brings back memories of my Scottish granny, Catherine Howe, who made a mean millionaire's shortbread. "A little bit of what you fancy does you no harm" was her motto and how right she was… the difficulty with this treat though is sticking to the "little bit" rule!

My modern twist is to incorporate a quality sea salt into the caramel, a flavor combination much loved by chocolate makers the world over.

SHORTBREAD
1 cup all-purpose flour
½ cup cornstarch
½ cup confectioners' sugar
1 stick unsalted butter, chilled and cubed

SALTED CARAMEL
1¼ cups packed light brown sugar
¾ cup heavy cream
6 tablespoons unsalted butter, softened
1 teaspoon crushed sea salt

CHOCOLATE TOPPING
7 oz. dark chocolate (70% cocoa solids)

a 9-inch square brownie pan, base and sides lined with a single piece of foil or baking parchment

Makes 16 squares

Either mix the shortbread ingredients together in a food processor or do it the traditional way by sifting the flour, cornstarch, and confectioners' sugar into a large bowl, adding the cubed butter and using clean fingertips to rub together until a dough forms.

Wrap the shortbread dough in plastic wrap and put in the fridge to rest for 1 hour. Press the rested dough into the prepared pan with your hands. Use the back of a spoon to flatten it.

Preheat the oven to 325°F.

Prick the top of the shortbread all over with a fork and bake in the preheated oven for about 40–45 minutes, until light brown and starting to come away from the edges of the pan. Allow to cool in the pan for at least 1 hour before you make the caramel.

To make the caramel, put the sugar and cream in a heavy-based saucepan and set over low heat. Heat gently, stirring with a wooden spoon as it comes to a boil. Once it is boiling, add the butter and stir.

Bring the caramel back to a boil and let it bubble gently for 5 minutes, stirring occasionally.

Take the caramel off the heat, add the salt, stir vigorously to ensure that it is thoroughly mixed in and then, working quickly, pour the caramel onto the cooled shortbread. Put the pan in the fridge for at least 1 hour to cool and set.

Once the caramel has set, melt the chocolate following the instructions for seed tempering given on page 14.

Pour the melted chocolate on top of the caramel and spread it evenly with a rubber spatula.

Leave the chocolate to set before lifting the shortbread out of the pan (using the foil or baking parchment) and cutting into squares with a hot knife.

The caramel squares will keep stored in an airtight container in the fridge for up to 3 days.

VERY BERRY CHEESECAKE BROWNIES

These brownies are a wonderful combination of fruity cheesecake on a chocolate base. They are very rich but quite delicious served as a special dessert or as mini sweet bites for a party.

BROWNIE BASE

7 oz. dark chocolate, chopped

1 stick plus 2 tablespoons unsalted butter, chilled and cut into pieces

3 eggs

3/4 cup granulated sugar

1/2 cup fine rice flour*

1/3 cup ground almonds*

CHEESECAKE TOPPING

10 oz. cream cheese, at room temperature

1/2 cup granulated sugar

2 eggs, beaten

1/2 teaspoon vanilla extract

1 cup mixed fresh berries, such as raspberries, blueberries, and blackberries

a 9-inch square brownie pan, base and sides lined with a single piece of foil

Makes 16 large squares or 30 mini bites

Preheat the oven to 325°F.

To make the brownie base, melt the chocolate and butter in a heatproof bowl set over a pan of barely simmering water. Once melted take the bowl off the heat and leave to cool for a few minutes.

Beat the eggs and sugar together in a separate bowl. Fold in the rice flour and ground almonds. Add the melted chocolate mixture and gently fold it all together.

Pour the mixture into the prepared pan and tap it on the work surface to ensure it is level.

To make the cheesecake topping, beat the cream cheese and sugar together in a bowl using a wooden spoon. Add the eggs and vanilla extract and mix in. (You may find it easier to use a handheld electric mixer to beat the mixture to a smooth and quite runny consistency.)

Pour the cheesecake mixture over the brownie base and push it into the corners with a palette knife or the back of a metal spoon.

Push the berries into the cheesecake, covering as much or as little of the surface as you wish.

Bake in the preheated oven for about 40–45 minutes, until risen, golden, and firm around the edges, but still pale in the middle and with a slight wobble.

Leave to cool in the pan for at least 2 hours then transfer the pan to the fridge to chill.

Use the foil lining to lift the chilled brownies out onto a chopping board and cut into squares with a hot knife. You may want to wipe the knife clean between each cut as it will be messy and doing so will keep each brownie square looking neat.

The brownies will keep stored in an airtight container in the fridge for up to 4 days, but do bring them back to room temperature before eating.

* **Note:** if preferred you can use 1 cup of all-purpose flour as an alternative to the rice flour and ground almonds.

SQUIDGY PECAN BROWNIES

My brownies are richer and softer than some classic recipes but are in fact low in sugar and gluten-free. I love the toffee notes of raw sugar and pecans, but you could quite easily replace the pecans with an equivalent weight of your favorite nuts or fruit and nut combinations; such as, dried cherries with walnuts, or macadamias with chopped stem ginger would be scrumptious here, too. Use this recipe as your brownie base to play with.

8 oz. dark chocolate, chopped
1 stick plus 2 tablespoons unsalted butter, chilled and cut into pieces
3 eggs
½ cup raw sugar
1 teaspoon vanilla extract
½ cup fine rice flour
¼ teaspoon crushed sea salt
1 cup shelled pecans, roughly chopped

a 9-inch square brownie pan, base and sides lined with a single piece of foil or baking parchment

Makes 12–16 brownies

Preheat the oven to 350°F.

Melt the chocolate and butter in a heatproof bowl set over a pan of barely simmering water. Once melted take the bowl off the heat and leave to cool for a few minutes.

Beat the eggs, sugar, and vanilla extract together in a separate bowl with a handheld electric mixer, until increased in volume, pale, and fluffy.

Fold the rice flour and salt into the egg and sugar mixture and then stir in the pecans, reserving a handful to scatter over the top. Add the melted chocolate and butter mixture and gently fold it all together.

Pour the mixture into the prepared pan and tap it on the work surface to ensure it is level. Scatter the reserved pecans over the top.

Bake in the preheated oven for about 15–17 minutes, until risen at the edges but still squidgy in the middle. Don't worry if it seems undercooked, as it will continue cooking after being taken out of the oven. Don't be tempted to overcook it or the brownies will be dry.

Leave to cool in the pan and then cut into squares of a size to suit you.

The brownies will keep stored in an airtight container for up to 3 days.

CRANBERRY & WHITE CHOCOLATE BROWNIES

"Intense", "squidgy", "moist", "yum", "wow" and "what's the recipe?" are just some of the reactions I get to these decadent little morsels and the best bit is that they are ridiculously easy to make. They are also gluten-free. No one would ever know that from eating them, and you will make anyone who cannot tolerate gluten, very happy indeed by baking these for them.

8 oz. dark chocolate, chopped
1 stick plus 2 tablespoons unsalted butter, chilled and cut into pieces
3 eggs
3/4 cup packed light brown sugar
1 teaspoon vanilla extract
1/2 cup fine rice flour
1/4 teaspoon crushed sea salt
1/3 cup dried cranberries
2 oz. white chocolate, chopped
sifted cocoa powder, to dust

a 9-inch square brownie pan, base and sides lined with a single piece of foil or baking parchment

Makes 16 brownies

Preheat the oven to 350°F.

Melt the dark chocolate and butter in a heatproof bowl set over a pan of barely simmering water. Once melted take the bowl off the heat and leave to cool for a few minutes.

Beat the eggs, sugar, and vanilla extract together in a large bowl with a handheld electric mixer, until increased in volume, pale, and fluffy.

Fold the rice flour and salt into the egg and sugar mixture and then stir in the cranberries and white chocolate.

Add the cooled chocolate and butter mixture and gently fold it all together.

Pour the mixture into the prepared pan and tap it on the work surface to ensure it is level.

Bake in the preheated oven for about 15–17 minutes, until risen at the edges but still squidgy in the middle. Don't worry if it seems undercooked, as it will continue cooking after being taken out of the oven. Don't be tempted to overcook it or the brownies will be dry.

Leave to cool in the pan, then dust with cocoa powder and cut into squares of a size to suit you. (They are very rich so you may want to cut smaller squares than normal.) The brownies will keep stored in an airtight container for up to 3 days.

STEPH'S CHOCOLATE BEET CAKE

This is a very special chocolate cake made by Steph Shepherd, who runs the locally famous Lobster Pot Café, below the Grand Hotel, at the north end of Swanage beach. It is the summer birthday party location of choice for many local children and no party or trip to the Lobster Pot is complete without enjoying Steph's equally famous cake. Steph likes to serve it piled high with fresh summer fruits and it is always demolished in minutes by young and old alike. The beets helps keep the sugar levels lower than other cakes and this cake is also butter-free, very moist, made with whole-wheat flour, and freezes well, either whole or in portions. There is no end to its talents!

9 oz. peeled cooked beets, chopped
1 teaspoon vanilla extract
3/4 cup safflower oil
3 eggs, beaten
1 1/2 cups white whole-wheat flour, sifted
2/3 cup cocoa powder, sifted
3/4 cup granulated sugar
1 1/2 teaspoons baking powder
3 cups mixed fresh berries, to top
sifted confectioners' sugar, to dust
sour cream or vanilla ice cream, to serve (optional)

a 9-inch springform cake pan, greased and base-lined with baking parchment

kitchen foil

Serves 8–10

Preheat oven to 350°F.

Purée the beets in a blender. Pour into a large bowl and add the vanilla extract, oil, and eggs. Mix together using a balloon whisk.

Sift the flour and cocoa powder into a separate large bowl and stir in the sugar and baking powder. Pour the beet mixture onto the dry ingredients and stir with a wooden spoon until blended.

Pour the mixture into the prepared pan and bake in the preheated oven for 30 minutes. After 30 minutes, remove the cake from the oven and put a foil "top hat" on top of it to prevent it from overbrowning. Return to the oven and cook for a further 10 minutes.

Remove the cake from the oven and leave it to cool in the pan—although it is also delicious served warm.

Pile the cake high with the berries and finish with a light dusting of sifted confectioners' sugar.

Serve with a dollop of sour cream or vanilla ice cream on the side, as preferred.

The cake will keep stored in an airtight container in the fridge for up to 4 days, or can be frozen for up to 1 month.

SCRUMPTIOUS CHOCOLATE CHUNK SCONES

This recipe is a domestic version of the Madagascan chocolate chunk scones made exclusively for us by the artisan bakers at the Winterborne Bakery, based in Winterborne Kingston, a village inland from us in Swanage. They make a lovely change from a classic scone, are easy to make and quite delicious served warm with fresh cream and cherry preserve or, as we like to serve them in our café, with dulce de leche caramel.

1³⁄₄ cups self-rising flour

2 tablespoon granulated sugar, plus extra for sprinkling

5 tablespoons unsalted butter, chilled and cut into pieces

2½ oz. dark chocolate (minimum 65% cocoa solids), chopped

2 eggs, beaten

3 tablespoons whole milk, plus more if required

TO SERVE

⅓ cup clotted cream or whipped heavy cream

cherry preserve, dulce de leche or Salted Caramel Sauce (see page 141)

a baking sheet, lightly greased

a 2½-inch fluted cutter

Makes about 10 scones

Preheat the oven to 425°F.

Put the flour in a large bowl and stir in the sugar. Add the butter and use your fingertips to rub the butter into the dry ingredients, until the mixture is crumbly.

Stir in the chocolate and then add half of the beaten egg, and the milk. Gently mix to form a dough—aim for a soft but not sticky consistency. You can gradually add more milk if necessary but do not overwork the dough or the scones will be tough.

When the dough clings together and forms a ball, turn it out onto a floured work surface. Use a rolling pin to roll out to a thickness of ½ inch.

Use the cutter to stamp out scones, rerolling the trimmings until you have used up all of the dough. Transfer to the prepared baking sheet.

Brush the tops of the scones with the remaining beaten egg and sprinkle each with a little sugar.

Bake in the preheated oven for 12–15 minutes, until well risen and lightly browned. Transfer to a wire rack to cool.

Serve while still warm with plenty of cream and cherry preserve, dulce de leche, or caramel sauce, as preferred.

The scones will keep stored in an airtight container for up to 2 days, or can be frozen for up to 2 weeks.

FRUITY CHOCOLATE FLAPJACKS

Full of energy-giving oats, fruits, dark chocolate, and zingy orange, these popular British treats known as flapjacks are perfect for lunchboxes, walking and camping expeditions, beach adventures, and picnics.

2 cups old-fashioned
    rolled oats
½ cup raisins
½ cup dried cranberries
finely grated peel of
    ½ an orange
3 oz. dark chocolate
    (70% cocoa solids),
    chopped
½ cup packed light
    brown sugar
1 stick unsalted butter,
    chilled and cubed
3 tablespoons freshly
    squeezed orange juice
3 tablespoons golden
    syrup or corn syrup

*a 9-inch square baking
pan, base-lined with
baking parchment*

Makes 12–16 flapjacks

Preheat the oven to 350°F.

Put the oats, raisins, cranberries, and grated orange peel in a large heatproof bowl and mix together.

Put the chocolate, sugar, butter, orange juice, and syrup into a large heavy-based saucepan and set over low heat. Melt, stirring occasionally until the sugar has dissolved.

Pour this mixture over the dry ingredients and stir to mix together.

Spoon the mixture into the prepared pan and level the surface with the back of a spoon. Bake in the preheated oven for 20 minutes, until browned around the outside edge and firm to the touch.

Leave the flapjacks to cool in the pan for about 10 minutes, then score the squares with a knife. Leave to cool completely before cutting.

The flapjacks will keep stored in an airtight container for up to 3 days.

COOKIES,
bars, & drinks

CHOCOLATE CHUNK COOKIES

I am a chocolate junkie, not a sugar addict, and I am constantly amazed at how much sugar is included in most cookie recipes, so my recipe here is relatively low in sugar but includes both semi-sweet and dark chocolates to give sweetness and flavor.

This is also an extremely easy and quick recipe to make using basic pantry ingredients, so is perfect for that domestic goddess moment, when a baked treat is called for after school or for unexpected visitors.

1 stick unsalted butter, at room temperature
1/3 cup packed light brown sugar
1 cup plus 3 tablespoons self-rising flour
1 tablespoon whole milk
1 teaspoon vanilla extract
2½ oz. dark chocolate (70% cocoa solids), chopped
2½ oz. semi-sweet chocolate (35% cocoa solids), chopped

2–3 baking sheets, lined with baking parchment

Makes 12 large cookies

Preheat the oven to 350°F.

Cream the butter and sugar together in a large bowl until light and fluffy. Add the flour and milk and mix into a dough.

Add the vanilla extract and chopped chocolates and stir into the mixture.

Use your hands to divide the dough into 12 balls. Arrange the balls on the prepared baking sheets, leaving plenty of space between each cookie as they will spread as they cook.

Squash each cookie gently with your fingers to make rounds about 2 inches in diameter (they will spread to about 3½ inches in diameter).

Bake in the preheated oven for 12–15 minutes, until golden brown.

Allow the cookies to cool and firm up on the baking sheets for a few minutes before transferring them to a wire rack.

Eat as soon as the cookies are cool enough to handle as they are at their most delicious when they are warm and the chocolate is still soft. If you do want to enjoy them later, I would advise gently warming them in a low oven for a few minutes to get that delicious "just-baked" taste.

The cookies will keep stored in an airtight container for up to 5 days, but they never last that long in our house!

CLAIRE'S TIP
For a quick dessert take a few cookies, warm them in the oven, pile some scoops of premium vanilla ice cream on top, and drizzle with a hot sauce (see recipes on page 141).

WHITE CHOCOLATE & FRESH RASPBERRY COOKIES

The flavors of fresh raspberries and white chocolate work brilliantly well together. This recipe is quick and easy to make and so tasty that you will be wanting to bake these cookies regularly!

1 stick unsalted butter, at room temperature
1/3 cup granulated sugar
1 cup plus 3 tablespoons self-rising flour
1 tablespoon whole milk
1 teaspoon vanilla extract
3 1/2 oz. white chocolate, chopped
1 scant cup fresh or frozen raspberries (if using frozen, allow them to soften for a few minutes before using)

3 baking sheets, lined with baking parchment

Makes 12 cookies

Preheat the oven to 350°F.

Cream the butter and sugar together in a bowl until light and fluffy. Add the flour and milk and mix into a dough.

Stir in the vanilla extract and chocolate. Mash the raspberries gently with a fork and stir them into the mixture. (This helps distribute the raspberries and also tinges the dough a lovely pink color.)

Use your hands to divide the dough into 12 balls. Arrange 4 balls on each prepared baking sheet, leaving plenty of space between them as the cookies will spread as they bake.

Shape each cookie very gently with your fingers to make chunky rounds about 2 inches in diameter (they will spread to about 3 1/2 inches in diameter).

Bake in the preheated oven for about 15 minutes, until golden brown.

Allow the cookies to cool and firm up on the baking sheets for a few minutes before transferring them to a wire rack.

Eat as soon as the cookies are cool enough to handle as they are definitely best eaten freshly baked and still warm.

If you do want to enjoy them later, warm the cookies gently in a low oven for a few minutes before eating for the best flavor.

As these cookies contain fresh fruit, they will be at their best for only 2–3 days, but somehow I don't think that they will be hanging around for too long!

CHILI, CHOCOLATE, & COCOA NIB COOKIES

These are grown-up cookies full of flavor and texture. The addition of cocoa nibs lifts them beyond the everyday, but if you cannot find cocoa nibs, the cookies are still deliciously tasty without them. Mini versions of these cookies also make a fabulous accompaniment to the Chocolate Fondue with Frozen Cherries on page 127.

1 stick unsalted butter, at room temperature
scant ½ cup raw sugar
1 cup plus 3 tablespoons self-rising flour
½ teaspoon ground cinnamon
½ teaspoon ancho chili powder
1 tablespoon whole milk
1 teaspoon vanilla extract
3½ oz. dark chocolate, roughly chopped
2½ tablespoons roasted cocoa nibs

2-3 baking sheets, lined with baking parchment

Makes about 14 large or 32 mini cookies

Preheat the oven to 350°F.

Cream the butter and sugar together in a large bowl until light and fluffy. Add the flour, cinnamon, chili powder, and milk and mix into a dough.

Add the vanilla extract, chocolate, and cocoa nibs and stir into the mixture.

Use your hands to divide the dough into 14 or 32 balls, depending on whether you are making large or mini cookies. Arrange the balls on the prepared baking sheets, leaving plenty of space between them as the cookies will spread during baking.

Squash each cookie gently with your fingers to make circles about ¼ inch in diameter for large or 1¼ inch in diameter for mini cookies (large ones will spread to about 3½ inches in diameter, mini ones won't spread as much). Bake in the preheated oven for about 12–15 minutes, until golden brown.

Allow the cookies to cool and firm up on the baking sheets for a few minutes before transferring them to a wire rack.

Eat as soon as the cookies are cool enough to handle, as they are delicious eaten warm while the chocolate is still soft. If you do want to eat them later, warm them in a low oven for a few minutes to get that "just-baked" taste.

The cookies will keep stored in an airtight container for 4–5 days, if you can resist them that long!

CARDAMOM, COFFEE, & CHOCOLATE COOKIES

This is another sophisticated cookie full of quality ingredients. The coffee adds a surprisingly subtle flavor, while the cardamom gives a lovely aromatic and warm spice note when you first bite into the cookie.

1 teaspoon instant coffee granules mixed with 3 tablespoons milk OR 1 tablespoon espresso mixed with 2 tablespoons milk

1 stick unsalted butter, at room temperature

½ cup raw sugar

1⅓ cups self-rising flour

seeds from 3 cardamom pods, finely crushed

3 oz. dark chocolate (70% cocoa solids), roughly chopped

2–3 baking sheets, lined with baking parchment

Makes about 12 large or 30 mini cookies

Preheat the oven to 350°F.

If using instant coffee, put the coffee in a small saucepan with the milk and warm gently to dissolve the coffee. Set aside until needed.

Cream the butter and sugar together in a large bowl with a handheld electric mixer until light and fluffy.

Add the flour, cardamom, and coffee mixture to the dough and mix in well. Stir in the chocolate.

Use your hands to divide the dough into 12 or 30 balls depending on whether you are making large or mini cookies. Arrange the balls on the prepared baking sheets, leaving plenty of space between them as the cookies will spread during baking.

Squash each cookie gently with your fingers to make circles about 2 inches in diameter for large or 1¼ inch in diameter for mini cookies (large ones will spread to about 3½ inches in diameter, mini ones won't spread as much). Bake in the preheated oven for 12–15 minutes, until golden brown.

Allow the cookies to cool and firm up on the baking sheets for a few minutes before transferring them to a wire rack.

Eat as soon as the cookies are cool enough to handle, as they are delicious eaten warm while the chocolate is still soft. If you do want to eat them later, warm them in a low oven for a few minutes to get that "just-baked" taste.

The cookies will keep stored in an airtight container for 4–5 days, if you can resist them that long!

ORANGE CHOCCIE DODGERS

This is a twist on the popular English cookie, the "Jammie Dodger" which is a shortcake filled with plum jam. My recipe has a chocolate filling and an orangey tang to the cookie. These look fantastic and make lovely handmade gifts, too. If you prefer, you can make the chocolate filling with all dark chocolate for adults or semi-sweet chocolate for children.

6½ tablespoons unsalted butter, softened

⅓ cup packed light brown sugar

1 egg, beaten

finely grated peel of 1 orange

1½ cups all-purpose flour

1 tablespoon cornstarch

1 teaspoon ground cinnamon

a pinch of salt

1½ oz. dark chocolate (70% cocoa solids), chopped

1½ oz. semi-sweet chocolate (minimum 35% cocoa solids), chopped

3 tablespoons heavy cream

a 3-inch and a 1¼-inch round cutter

2 baking sheets, lined with baking parchment

Makes 10–15 cookies

Cream the butter and sugar together in a bowl with a handheld electric mixer until light and fluffy. Add the egg and grated orange peel. Sift in the flour, cornstarch, and cinnamon and add the salt. Use your hands to knead into a dough.

Wrap the dough in plastic wrap and put in the fridge to rest for 30 minutes.

Preheat the oven to 350°F.

Roll out the rested dough very thinly on a lightly floured work surface. Use the larger cutter to stamp out an even number of shapes. Use the smaller cutter to stamp out a hole in the center of half of these shapes. (If you like, you can cook these cut-out shapes separately to make mini cookies to serve with ice cream or a chocolate fondue.)

Use a metal spatula to carefully lift the shapes onto the baking sheets, leaving some space between each one as the cookies will spread as they cook.

Bake in the preheated oven for about 10 minutes, until golden. Use a metal spatula to transfer the cookies to a wire rack and leave to cool completely.

To make the ganache, put the chocolates and cream in a heatproof bowl set over a saucepan of barely simmering water. Stir continuously until the chocolate has melted and blended with the cream.

When the cookies are completely cool, spread a little of the warm chocolate ganache onto the complete cookies and stick the ones with cut-out holes on top.

Leave the finished cookies to set for at least 15 minutes before eating.

These cookies will keep stored in an airtight container in the fridge for up to 2 days.

DOUBLE CHOCOLATE SHORTBREAD

These melt-in-the-mouth shortbreads use confectioners' sugar rather than granulated sugar to give them a much smoother texture than a more traditional recipe. The dough can be made ahead, kept in the fridge overnight and then rolled out and baked as required. Why not make these suitable for special or seasonal occasions by varying the shape of cookie cutters used? If you want to decorate them some more, add some sugar strands, or colorful sprinkles after dipping and before the chocolate has set firm.

¾ cup all-purpose flour
½ cup cornstarch
½ cup confectioners' sugar
3 tablespoons cocoa powder
1 stick unsalted butter, chilled and cubed

TO DECORATE
4 oz. dark chocolate (70% cocoa solids) or semi-sweet chocolate (35% cocoa solids)
sugar strands or other sprinkles (optional)

2 baking sheets, lined with baking parchment

a 3-inch round cutter

Makes 10–15 cookies

Sift the flour, cornstarch, confectioners' sugar, and cocoa powder into a large bowl and add the butter.

Gradually form a dough by rubbing the flour mixture and butter together with your fingertips. It will begin to form crumbs and then after a few minutes you will be able to knead it into a dough.

Wrap the dough in plastic wrap and put in the fridge to rest for at least 1 hour.

Preheat the oven to 250°F.

Bring the dough back to room temperature and roll out on a lightly floured work surface. Alternatively, try the "plastic wrap method." Using this method means you don't need to flour the surface and can move your shapes onto the baking sheet more easily. To do this, place the dough between two loose sheets of plastic wrap, roll out thinly and then peel the top layer of plastic wrap away.

Use the cutter to stamp out the shapes (leaving enough space around each one as they will spread during baking), then, leaving everything in situ, take the opposite edges of the plastic wrap, lift the whole sheet and turn it upside down onto your baking sheet. Lift off the plastic wrap, then the excess dough around the cut-out shapes and *voila!*

Bake in the preheated oven for about 45 minutes. Transfer to a wire rack and let cool completely.

To decorate, melt 3 oz. of the chocolate in a heatproof bowl set over a saucepan of barely simmering water. Once melted, remove the bowl from the pan and stir in the remaining chocolate until melted.

Dip each cooled cookie in the melted chocolate (either just half or all over, as preferred) and decorate with sprinkles if liked. Put each cookie on the second baking sheet as you work. Transfer to the fridge and leave the chocolate to set.

The shortbreads will keep stored in an airtight container and layered with baking parchment for 4–5 days.

VARIATION
For a variation, you can use this recipe to make plain shortbreads. Simply omit the cocoa powder and increase the quantity of flour to 1 cup.

LUKULLUS

This is another Christmas recipe from my childhood, given to me by a friend with a German mother. A simple tiered stack of crunchy thin almond cookies, layered with a rich dark chocolate paste. It is a no-cook recipe simple enough for a child to make, but is surprisingly "moreish", as my mum would say.

1½ sticks unsalted butter
¾ cup cocoa powder, plus extra to dust
¾ cup superfine sugar
1 egg
7 oz. almond thins, thin butter cookies or *langue-de-chat* cookies
sifted cocoa powder, to dust
sifted confectioners' sugar, to dust

an 8 x 4 x 2½-inch loaf pan, lined with a single piece of foil or a baking parchment loaf pan liner

Makes 12 thin slices

Melt the butter in a saucepan set over low heat. Once melted, sift in the cocoa powder and stir until blended and smooth. Leave to cool for a few minutes.

Cream the sugar and egg together in a large bowl. Add the melted butter and cocoa mixture and mix to make a smooth chocolate paste.

To assemble the lukullus, start by spreading a thick layer of chocolate paste at the bottom of the prepared pan, then add a layer of cookies, then a thinner layer of paste. Repeat until all of the cookies and chocolate paste have been used, finishing with a layer of chocolate paste. You should be able to make at least 7–8 layers of cookies. Put in the fridge and leave to chill for at least 1 hour.

Invert the loaf pan and turn the lukullus out onto a serving plate. Remove the foil and dust the top with sifted cocoa powder and confectioners' sugar.

To serve, use a serrated knife to cut into thin slices.

This is best eaten on the day it is made as it contains raw egg (see note on page 4), but if you don't manage to munch it all at once, store in an airtight container in the fridge.

MARBLED GINGER BARS

This is one of the most popular no-cook bars that we serve in Cocoa Central, our café at Chococo HQ. It is my adaptation of an old family recipe and reminds me of helping my mum make chocolate treats for Christmas.
It won us a 2-star Gold Great Taste Award in 2008 and remains a bestseller.

6 oz. old-fashioned gingersnaps (about 25 small cookies)

1 stick unsalted butter

7 oz. dark chocolate (70% cocoa solids), broken into pieces

1 tablespoon superfine sugar

2 tablespoons golden syrup or corn syrup

⅓ cup chopped crystalized ginger

TOPPING

7 oz. dark chocolate, chopped

2 oz. semi-sweet chocolate, chopped

an 11 x 7- inch jelly roll pan or a 9-inch square brownie pan, lined with foil

Makes 12 bars or 24 mini bites

Crush the cookies into small pieces. The easiest way to do this is to put them in a polythene bag and bash with a rolling pin, but not too much as you do want pieces not crumbs.

Put the butter, dark chocolate, sugar, and syrup in a large heavy-based saucepan and set over low heat. Let melt, stirring continuously.

Take off the heat, add the crushed cookies and ginger and mix well until everything is coated in the chocolate mixture. Pour the mixture into the prepared pan and transfer to the fridge to set.

To make the topping, seed temper the dark chocolate following the instructions given on page 14. Pour the chocolate over the chilled mixture, spreading it over the surface with a metal spatula. Return to the fridge to set before decorating.

To decorate, melt the semi-sweet chocolate in a heatproof bowl set over a saucepan of barely simmering water.

When just melted remove the bowl from the heat. Dip the tines of a fork into the melted chocolate and holding it above the pan, move it backwards and forwards to drizzle the chocolate in a random pattern over the top of the bars.

Return to the fridge to set the semi-sweet chocolate and then cut into bars with a hot serrated knife.

The bars will keep stored in an airtight container in the fridge for up to 3 weeks.

VARIATION

To make Original Marbled Bars, simply follow the main recipe above, replacing the ginger cookies with graham crackers, or similar, and using 1¼ cup raisins or a mixture of any chopped dried fruits and nuts instead of the crystalized ginger. To top, follow the main recipe.

INDULGENT HOT CHOCOLATE

Similar to those served in our chocolate café, this is a hot chocolate with bells and whistles on! We serve these in French-style bowls so that you can cup both hands around it.

3 oz. dark chocolate (70% cocoa solids and preferably Venezuelan), chopped
2 cups whole or low-fat milk, as preferred
1 teaspoon sugar, or more to taste
2 tablespoons whipped cream

a large handful of white mini marshmallows
dark chocolate curls (see page 15)
a handful of chocolate-covered malt balls

2 serving cups

Serves 2

Put the chopped chocolate and 4 tablespoons of the milk in a small heavy-based saucepan and warm gently to melt the chocolate into the milk.

Use a small whisk to stir this mixture into a smooth paste and once you are happy that the chocolate has all melted, only then add the rest of the milk and the sugar.

Bring to a boil stirring all the time. The moment it reaches a boil, take off the heat and whisk vigorously for a minute to make a foam.

Pour your foaming hot chocolate into 2 serving cups, top each with a spoonful of whipped cream, marshmallows, chocolate curls, and finally the malt balls. Add more sugar if you feel the drinks need it.

Serve immediately with a spoon.

HOT CHOCOLATE BERG

Although I believe the technical term for this particular confection is a "float", we have found in our café here at Chococo, that the ice cream tends to float mostly under the surface in an iceberg-like fashion, which is why we call it a 'berg!

1 3/4 cups whole or low-fat milk, as preferred
2 1/2 oz. dark chocolate (70% cocoa solids), chopped
1 teaspoon sugar, or more to taste

2 scoops vanilla or coffee ice cream, as preferred
milk or dark chocolate curls (see page 15)

2 serving cups

Serves 2

Put the chopped chocolate and 4 tablespoons of the milk into a small heavy-based saucepan and warm gently to melt the chocolate into the milk.

Use a small whisk to stir this mixture into a smooth paste and once you are happy that the chocolate has all melted, only then add the rest of the milk and the sugar.

Bring to a boil stirring all the time. The moment it reaches a boil, take off the heat and whisk vigorously for a minute to make a foam.

Fill 2 serving cups two-thirds full with the foaming hot chocolate, carefully add a scoop of ice cream, and then top up with the remaining hot chocolate. (This allows for varying cup sizes and prevents any spillages as you put the ice cream in.)

Sprinkle some chocolate curls on top and serve immediately with a spoon.

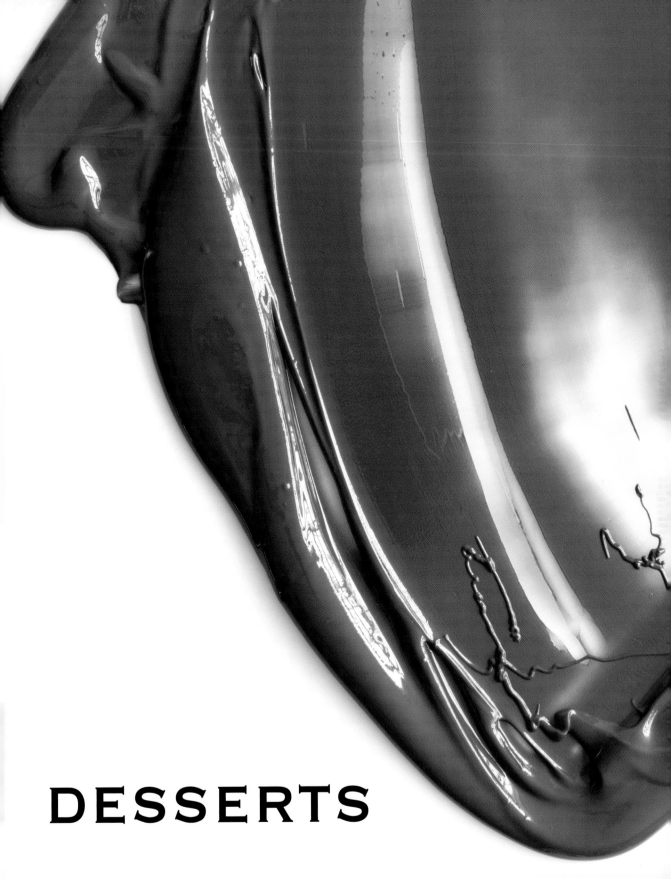

DESSERTS

NUTMEG-SPICED CHOCOLATE CHEESECAKE

I created this cheesecake after a wonderful trip to Grenada, the Isle of Spice (and cocoa!), with a little help from my daughter Lily who suggested that to make it even more chocolatey, I melt dark chocolate into the crumb crust and it really works. Do use freshly grated nutmeg as this is what really gives it an aromatic flavor. It is delicious served as it is, or topped with tropical fruits to help transport you to that sweet-smelling island in the Caribbean.

CRUMB CRUST

3½ tablespoons unsalted butter

2 oz. dark chocolate (preferably 71% cocoa solids from the Grenada Chocolate Company), chopped

6 oz. graham crackers or digestive biscuits

CHEESECAKE

4 oz. white chocolate, chopped

14 oz. cream cheese, at room temperature

⅔ cup sour cream

¾ cup granulated sugar

3 eggs, lightly beaten plus 2 egg yolks

2–3 teaspoons freshly grated nutmeg

fresh tropical fruits of your choice, such as mango, passion fruit, and papaya (optional)

an 8-inch springform cake pan, base-lined with baking parchment and wrapped in a watertight layer of foil

a roasting pan, large enough to take the cake pan

Serves 8

To make the crumb crust, melt the butter and chocolate together in a saucepan set over very low heat.

Crush the crackers to a fine crumb, either in a food processor, or put them in a polythene bag and bash with a rolling pin.

Add the cracker crumbs to the melted chocolate and butter mixture and stir until thoroughly coated. Transfer the mixture to the prepared pan and press down firmly using your hand or the back of a spoon. Put in the fridge to cool and firm up.

Preheat the oven to 325°F.

To make the cheesecake, melt the white chocolate in a heatproof bowl set over a saucepan of barely simmering water.

Once the white chocolate has melted, take the bowl off the heat and leave to cool for 5 minutes.

Beat the cream cheese and sour cream in a bowl until smooth, then stir in the sugar and the eggs. Add the cooled white chocolate and the grated nutmeg. (This may seem a lot of nutmeg but any less and the flavor doesn't quite come through.)

Put the cake pan into the roasting pan and pour the cheesecake mixture over the crumb crust. Pour in enough hot water to come halfway up the sides of the pan. Carefully transfer to the oven.

Bake in the preheated oven for about 40–50 minutes, until set around the edges but still a little wobbly in the center—it will finish setting as it cools.

Remove the cheesecake from the oven and let cool slightly before putting in the fridge to chill for at least 1 hour.

When ready to serve, remove from the pan and top with the tropical fruits, if using. Use a hot knife to slice.

CHOCOLATE PANCAKES PLATTER

One of my favorite appetizers is a platter of "blini" pancakes served with a selection of savory toppings to pick and choose from. I have taken this idea to new heights and created a recipe for a fun chocolate dessert! Here little chocolate pancakes are served with a homemade cherry compote, sour cream, and toasted almonds, but they are also good with fresh berries or sliced bananas, dulce de leche caramel and pecans or hazelnuts for the kids.

CHERRY COMPOTE
8 oz. fresh cherries, pitted and halved
2 tablespoons granulated sugar
finely grated peel of ½ a lemon
2 tablespoons red wine or kirsch

PANCAKES
1 cup plus 2 tablespoons self-rising flour
¼ cup cocoa powder
2 tablespoons granulated sugar
1 egg, beaten
¾ cup whole milk
1 tablespoon unsalted butter, melted

TO SERVE
sifted confectioners' sugar, to dust
cherry compote (see above) or fresh berries
sour cream
toasted slivered almonds

Makes about 30 mini pancakes

To make the cherry compote, put the cherries, sugar, and grated lemon peel in a saucepan and warm over gentle heat. Once the sugar dissolves and the cherries start to release their juices, add the wine or kirsch and simmer gently for about 5–7 minutes, until the cherries are soft, but still holding their shape and the liquid has reduced and thickened slightly. The cherries and wine should produce a good amount of liquid, but if it does start to look a bit dry, add a little water. Leave to cool before serving.

To make the pancakes, sift the flour and cocoa together into a mixing bowl and add the sugar. Mix the egg, milk, and melted butter together and add this mixture to the dry ingredients. Beat together to make a thick and creamy batter. Cover and let rest for at least 30 minutes before using.

Heat a heavy-based skillet, lightly grease with butter and wipe away any excess with paper towels.

Drop dessertspoonfuls of the mixture into the hot skillet—each one should spread out to make a pancake about 2 inches in diameter. Turn the pancakes over as bubbles start to appear and briefly cook on other side.

Remove the pancakes from the skillet with a fish slice and either serve immediately or keep warm, wrapped in a clean kitchen towel in a low oven, until required.

Serve on a large platter, dusted with confectioners' sugar and surrounded by small dishes of cherry compote or fresh berries, sour cream, and slivered almonds, or any other combination of toppings that you like.

Any uncooked pancake batter will keep covered in the fridge overnight, but may need beating and thinning with a little milk before cooking.

WHITE CHOCOLATE, OATMEAL, & BERRY CRANACHAN

This dessert is my twist on the classic Scottish dessert cranachan, which combines raspberries with whisky and oatmeal. My interpretation combines a Drambuie-infused white chocolate fresh cream ganache with mixed berries and a crunchy toasted oatmeal brittle, for three very different but complementary tastes and textures... delicious!

½ cup pinhead oatmeal or Irish oatmeal (not rolled oats)

½ cup granulated sugar

5½ oz. white chocolate, chopped

½ cup whipping cream

2 tablespoons Drambuie or whisky, plus a little extra for the berries (optional)

1⅓ cups fresh or frozen mixed berries

4 glasses or dessert dishes

a baking sheet, lined with baking parchment

Serves 4

Toast the oatmeal in a dry non-stick skillet until brown, shaking the pan regularly to ensure the oatmeal toasts evenly and does not burn.

Put the sugar in a small heavy-based saucepan and melt slowly over low heat, stirring occasionally—watch it closely to ensure that it doesn't burn. As soon as the sugar has melted, add half of the toasted oatmeal to the skillet and stir in.

Working quickly, pour the oatmeal and sugar mixture over the prepared baking sheet. Leave to set at room temperature. Once set, put the brittle into an airtight bag or container (to keep it away from moisture) until required.

Melt the white chocolate in a bowl set over a pan of barely simmering water.

While the chocolate is melting, put the cream in a saucepan and bring to a boil. Take off the heat, let cool slightly and pour into the melting chocolate. Stir until blended. Once the chocolate and cream have blended, take the bowl off the heat, add the Drambuie and remaining toasted oatmeal and stir in.

Leave the white chocolate ganache to cool and then transfer to the fridge for about 30 minutes.

If using frozen fruit, take the berries out of the freezer to defrost while the ganache is cooling. If you are using fresh fruits, reserve a few attractive pieces of fruit for decoration and lightly mash the rest with a fork. You can add a little drambuie to the mashed fruit, if liked. (I don't add any sugar to the fruit, as I love the contrast of the tart fruit with the sweet white chocolate cream, but do add a little sugar to yours if liked.) Remove the white chocolate ganache from the fridge. It will still be quite runny so beat it with a handheld electric mixer for 2–3 minutes, until light, airy, and mousse-like.

To assemble the desserts, divide the berries between the serving glasses, then top up with generous spoonfuls of the white chocolate ganache. Top each serving with the reserved fresh berries and a piece of oatmeal brittle. Serve immediately.

CROWNS OF PASSION

These regal chocolate crowns, filled with a mousse-like white chocolate ganache, fresh fruits, and passion fruit syrup, look fabulous, are surprisingly easy to make and can be adapted to suit your taste, the seasons, a special event and so on. The crowns, ganache, and syrup can all be made the day ahead and will keep in the fridge until required.

7 oz. dark chocolate (70% cocoa solids), chopped

4 sheets of edible gold leaf (optional)

4 physalis (cape gooseberries)

1 cup strawberries, raspberries, and blueberries, or any other fresh fruit of your choice

WHITE CHOCOLATE GANACHE FILLING

⅓ cup crème fraîche or heavy cream

3½ oz. white chocolate

PASSION FRUIT SYRUP

¼ cup granulated sugar

4 ripe passion fruit

a pastry brush

5 ramekins (maximum 3¼ inches diameter) or small pudding molds, lined with foil

a small paintbrush (optional)

Serves 4

To make the crowns, melt the dark chocolate in a heatproof bowl set over a saucepan of barely simmering water. Do not let the base of the bowl touch the water. Once melted, remove the bowl from the heat.

Use a pastry brush to paint the inside of the prepared ramekins with melted chocolate, taking the chocolate about 1½ inches up the sides and aiming for a "filigree" top edge. You will need to apply 3 coats of chocolate, so put the ramekins in the fridge for a few minutes in between applying each coat. Put the bowl of chocolate back onto the pan of barely simmering water if it becomes too thick to work with. Don't worry if the chocolate "blooms" inside the ramekin as you will be filling them to the brim.

Leave the chocolate crowns to set for at least 1 hour before gently peeling away the foil. It may be tricky to remove in places but it will peel off. (The reason I have suggested preparing 5 crowns is to give you a back-up in case one breaks!)

A small paintbrush is very useful to help you stick the gold leaf onto the crowns, or to move it around—be prepared for it to stick to everything, including your fingers! Put the decorated chocolate crowns on a baking sheet and store in the fridge until needed.

To make the white chocolate ganache, warm the crème fraîche or cream in a heavy-based saucepan set over low heat until just boiling. Take the pan off the heat and add the chopped white chocolate, stirring until melted. Put the pan back on the heat if necessary to melt the chocolate completely. Take off the heat and leave to cool completely before putting in the fridge for at least 1 hour.

To make the syrup, put a generous ⅓ cup cold water in a small heavy-based saucepan, add the sugar and heat gently until the sugar has dissolved. Turn up the heat and simmer for about 5 minutes, until the syrup changes color and reduces in volume. Add the pulp of the passion fruits and boil for a further 3 minutes. Let cool.

Once cool, pour the syrup into a pitcher through a strainer to remove the pips (or leave them in if preferred). Store in the fridge until required.

When ready to assemble, take the ganache out of the fridge and whisk for 2–3 minutes with a handheld electric mixer, until soft and mousse-like. Put the chocolate crowns on serving plates. Divide the ganache between them and arrange some fresh fruit in each, drizzle with a little passion fruit syrup and serve immediately.

WILD THING CHOCOLATE FONDANTS

4½ oz. dark chocolate
  (70% cocoa solids,
  preferably with
  berry fruit notes)
6½ tablespoons unsalted
  butter
3 eggs
½ cup packed light
  brown sugar
⅓ cup all-purpose flour
20 Griottine® cherries in
  kirsch syrup or similar
sifted confectioners'
  sugar, to dust
vanilla ice cream or
  sour cream, to serve

*four ½-cup capacity
dariole or pudding molds,
brushed generously with
melted butter and lightly
dusted with cocoa powder*

Serves 4

Melt the chocolate and butter in a heatproof bowl set over a saucepan of barely simmering water. Do not let the base of the bowl touch the water. Once the chocolate has melted, take the bowl off the heat and set aside to cool for a few minutes.

Put the eggs and sugar in a large grease-free bowl and use a handheld electric mixer to beat until thick, pale, and fluffy.

Fold the cooled chocolate and butter mixture into the egg and sugar mixture, then sift in the flour and gently fold in.

Put 2 heaping tablespoons of the mixture in each prepared mold and chill for at least 30 minutes. Remove from the fridge and put 5 cherries and ½ teaspoon kirsch syrup into each one. Add another 2 tablespoons of the fondant mixture to each mold.

Cover and return the molds to the fridge for at least 1 hour. They can be chilled for several hours or overnight.

Preheat the oven to 400°F. When you are ready to bake, make sure that the oven has reached the right temperature.

Put the molds on a baking sheet and into the preheated oven to bake for exactly 11 minutes, until gently risen, starting to form a crust on top, and coming away from the edges of the molds. (If you cook them for less time, the fondants will collapse when you take them out of the molds, and if you cook them for any longer, they will be a firmer chocolate dessert with a less molten center... but they will still taste delicious so don't worry too much if this happens!)

Remove the fondants from the oven and let rest in the molds for 1 minute. It's best to wear an oven glove to handle the molds as they will be very hot. Put a serving plate on top of a mold and carefully turn it upside down. The mold should lift off the fondant easily, assuming you buttered them well enough. If you are nervous, it's fine to serve them in the molds.

Serve immediately, lightly dusted with confectioners' sugar and with vanilla ice cream or sour cream on the side.

The fondants can be frozen for up to 2 weeks (uncooked and in their molds) but defrost fully before baking.

My version of this popular and indulgent dessert takes its inspiration from our "Wild Thing" cherry chocolate, which is a kirsch-marinated morello cherry nestled in the middle of a rich dark chocolate ganache.

You can buy these marinated cherries in delicatessens, but if you cannot find them, you could make the cherry compote on page 99 for an equally scrumptious alternative, or if preferred, three fresh raspberries and half a teaspoon of framboise liqueur in each fondant is also delicious.

PARADISO CHOCOLATE PÂTÉ

This brings back memories of the BT Global Challenge Round the World yacht race, which I took part in back in 1996/7 and of our New Zealand stopover. I spent two very happy weeks with a gang of friends from other yachts touring South Island doing as many high adrenalin adventures as we could and eating fabulous food in cafés tucked away in tiny towns. This is my adaptation of a recipe from the Café Paradiso in Wellington and makes a very special and grown-up dessert that is a twist on a savory pâté.

¾ cup dried apricots (ideally sundried), chopped

¾ cup pitted prunes, chopped

⅓ cup raisins

⅓ cup alcohol of your choice (as a sailor, I like to use dark rum but you can use brandy, Cointreau, or whisky)

14 oz. dark chocolate (70% cocoa solids), chopped

6½ tablespoons unsalted butter

3 egg yolks

3 tablespoons heavy cream

TO SERVE
butter cookies, almond or ginger thins, or plain shortbread
fresh figs, dates, or grapes

a 9 x 5 x 3-inch loaf pan, lined with a single piece of foil or a baking parchment loaf pan liner

Serves 8–10

Put the apricots, prunes, and raisins in a non-reactive bowl and cover with the alcohol. Leave to marinate for at least 1 hour, longer if possible.

Melt the chocolate and the butter in a heatproof bowl set over a saucepan of barely simmering water.

When melted, take the bowl off the heat and stir in the egg yolks, one at a time. As the mixture is warm, the eggs will gently cook at the same time.

Add the cream and stir gently to blend it all together. Let the mixture cool for about 30 minutes.

When cool, stir in the marinated dried fruit and any marinating liquid.

Pour the mixture into the prepared loaf pan and level the surface with a rubber spatula. Cover with another piece of foil and chill in the fridge until set, ideally overnight to give the flavors time to mature. You can leave it for a couple of days if you wish, if anything, the flavors just get better!

When ready to serve, remove the pâté from the fridge. Turn it out onto a serving plate and leave for at least 30 minutes to bring it back to room temperature. Cut into thin slices with a hot knife and put 2 slices of pâté on each serving plate, along with several cookies and fresh fruit of your choice.

STICKY TOFFEE CHOCCIE PUDDINGS

PUDDINGS

2 cups dried pitted dates, preferably Medjool or halawi, chopped

1 teaspoon baking soda

1 cup freshly brewed breakfast tea

5 tablespoons unsalted butter, softened

3/4 cup dark brown sugar

2 eggs, beaten

1 teaspoon vanilla extract

1 1/3 cups self-rising flour

1 tablespoon cocoa powder

1 teaspoon apple pie spice

vanilla ice cream, to serve

CHOCOLATE TOFFEE SAUCE

1 cup heavy cream

6 1/2 tablespoons unsalted butter

1/2 dark brown sugar

1 oz. dark chocolate, finely chopped

a 12-cup muffin pan, lined with paper muffin cases

Makes 12 puddings

To make the puddings, put the chopped dates and baking soda in the tea and leave for 20 minutes, ideally longer if you have time.

Preheat the oven to 350°F.

Cream the butter and sugar together in a mixing bowl, until light and fluffy, using either a handheld electric mixer or a wooden spoon. Add the beaten eggs and vanilla extract and mix well.

Sift the flour, cocoa powder, and apple pie spice into the bowl and mix until combined. Add the tea-soaked dates to the mixture along with any remaining soaking juice. The batter will be quite sloppy at this point, but don't worry, it is supposed to be!

Divide the mixture between the muffin cases and bake in the preheated oven for 20–25 minutes, until risen and brown and a skewer inserted in the center comes out clean.

To make the chocolate toffee sauce, put the cream, butter, sugar, and chocolate in a heavy-based saucepan and set over low heat. Stir until the butter and chocolate have melted, the sugar has dissolved and you have a smooth sauce.

Remove the paper cases from the warm puddings, put them on serving plates and prick the top of each one all over with a toothpick—this will help the sauce soak into the sponge cake. Spoon the warm sauce all over the puddings and drizzle some around them. The puddings are best served with a scoop of vanilla ice cream on the side.

The puddings will keep stored in an airtight container for 2–3 days and the sauce for at least a week (if covered and refrigerated) so can be made ahead if required.

Sticky toffee "pudding" is a classic British baked dessert and one of my favorites, but it can often lack flavor and be disappointing. Soaking the dates in tea, using dark brown sugar, and adding a touch of apple pie spice and a dash of cocoa powder to the mixture all add a certain something and make this recipe rather special. As if that wasn't enough, the toffee sauce also boasts a hint of rich dark chocolate.

GORGEOUS GINGER CHOCOLATE MOUSSE

This recipe really couldn't be simpler and always surprises people when I tell them that you can make a mousse with just chocolate and water!

It is very rich and dense, so a very small serving will go a long way. I add tiny chunks of stem ginger to give texture, heat, and a touch of sweetness all in one to this very pure mousse. It a great dessert for anyone who doesn't eat dairy.

4½ oz. dark chocolate, (minimum 60% cocoa solids), chopped
½ cup freshly boiled water
1½ tablespoons finely chopped stem ginger
1 teaspoon stem ginger syrup
sifted cocoa powder, to dust

espresso cups, egg cups, or similar

Serves 6

Put the chocolate in a heatproof bowl set over a saucepan of barely simmering water and melt gently. Do not let the base of the bowl touch the water.

Once the chocolate has melted, add the water in thirds (do not add the water while it is still boiling as it may scorch the chocolate). Stir continuously. The mixture is very runny at this point but don't worry, it will thicken as it cools.

Add 1 tablespoon of the chopped stem ginger and the syrup to the chocolate and stir. Pour the mixture into a lipped pitcher and then pour into espresso cups. (Using a lipped pitcher means you will be able to fill the cups easily without it dripping everywhere!)

Put the mousses on a tray or baking sheet and carefully transfer to the fridge to set for at least 1 hour.

When ready to serve, bring the mousses back to room temperature, scatter a little of the remaining chopped stem ginger on top of each one, and dust with sifted cocoa powder. Serve immediately.

VARIATION
If you would like a slightly sweeter version of this mousse and are happy to include dairy, you can make it with a combination of 2½ oz. dark chocolate and 2 oz. semi-sweet chocolate. This mousse will set a little softer.

BALSAMIC BERRY CHOCOLATE MOUSSE

This is a chocolate mousse that takes its inspiration from our popular "Balsamic Berry" summer chocolate, in that it blends the classic combination of balsamic vinegar with berries, together with dark chocolate. Please don't compromise on the quality of the balsamic vinegar you use.

¾ cup fresh strawberries
¾ cup fresh raspberries
1 teaspoon confectioners' sugar
5½ oz. dark chocolate, (60–70% cocoa solids and ideally from Madagascar), chopped
5 tablespoons softened unsalted butter
2 egg yolks
1 tablespoon aged balsamic vinegar
3 egg whites
2 tablespoons superfine sugar
sifted confectioners' sugar, to dust

6 espresso cups or similar

Serves 6

Wash and pat dry the berries, selecting some attractive ones to reserve for decoration. Use a fork to lightly mash the remaining berries with the confectioners' sugar. Put a tablespoonful in the bottom of each serving cup and set aside.

Put the chocolate in a heatproof bowl set over a saucepan of barely simmering water. Do not let the base of the bowl touch the water. As soon as the chocolate has melted, take the bowl off the heat. Add the butter and stir until melted. Add the egg yolks and the balsamic vinegar.

In a separate grease-free bowl, whisk the egg whites with a handheld electric mixer until softly peaking. Add the sugar and whisk again until firmly peaking. Gently fold the whisked egg whites into the chocolate and butter mixture. A light touch is needed here—if you beat it too much you will lose the air in the egg whites. Ensure you pick up all the chocolate mixture at the bottom of the bowl as you fold the two mixtures together.

Carefully spoon the mousse into each serving cup, on top of the mashed berries. Put the mousses in the fridge to set for at least 1 hour.

Take the mousses out of the fridge and let return to room temperature. Decorate with the reserved fruit and dust with sifted confectioners' sugar to serve.

BLACKSTRAP HARRY TART WITH RUM-SOZZLED RAISINS

This gorgeous dessert tart, with its hint of rich blackstrap molasses blended with dark chocolate, is based on our award-winning "Blackstrap Harry" chocolate. If you are wondering about the name, we think that blackstrap molasses is a very piratical sounding ingredient, so our chocolate, and this tart, is named after Harry, a local Purbeck pirate of old who has the famous Old Harry rocks, just north of Swanage Bay, named after him.

SOZZLED RAISINS

1 cup large raisins, preferably Lexia or Chilean flame

freshly squeezed juice of ½ an orange

3 strips of orange peel

8 tablespoons dark rum

1 tablespoon light brown sugar

TART CRUST

7 oz. all-butter shortbread cookies

5 tablespoons unsalted butter, melted

½ tablespoon light brown sugar

GANACHE FILLING

9 oz. dark chocolate (70% cocoa solids), chopped

1¼ cups heavy cream

1 tablespoon blackstrap molasses

½ cup packed light brown sugar

½ teaspoon sea salt

an 8-inch loose-based cake pan, base and sides lined with baking parchment

Serves 8

To prepare the sozzled raisins, put them in a small saucepan, along with the orange juice and grated peel, and 6 tablespoons of the rum. Bring to a boil then set aside to cool and allow the raisins to plump up, ideally for several hours.

To make the tart crust, crush the cookies to a very fine crumb, either in a food processor or put them in a strong polythene bag and bash with a rolling pin.

Melt the butter in a saucepan set over low heat. Add the cookie crumbs and sugar and stir to combine. Transfer the mixture to the prepared cake pan and press down firmly into the base. Chill in the fridge until required.

To make the ganache, put the chocolate in a heatproof bowl set over a saucepan of gently simmering water. Do not allow the base of the bowl to touch the water.

Put the cream, molasses, sugar, and salt in a heavy-based saucepan and set over medium heat. Stir continuously as it slowly comes to a boil and the sugar dissolves completely.

Pour the hot cream mixture onto the chocolate and stir until the chocolate has melted. If it doesn't all melt, don't worry, sit the bowl over the pan of gently simmering water for a little longer until the chocolate does fully melt. Take the bowl off the pan and set aside to cool for at least 30 minutes.

Once the ganache filling is cool, pour it onto the chilled tart crust. Transfer to the fridge to set.

Just before serving, take the now-plump raisins out of their marinade and set aside. Remove the orange peel and add the sugar and the remaining 2 tablespoons rum to the marinade. Boil for a few minutes until thickened and syrupy. I would highly recommend tasting your syrup at this point to tweak it to your taste before pouring it into a small pitcher.

Use a hot knife to cut slices from the tart and serve with the sozzled raisins and syrup spooned over the top.

APRICOT AND AMARETTI MASCARPONE TARTLETS

Naturally sundried apricots are dark in color and have a deliciously intense fruity taste that mass-produced, bright orange colored apricots just don't have. I love these tartlets, as they marry the apricots with chocolate and amaretti cookies with delicious results, and are also very easy to make.

1 cup naturally sundried apricots
3½ oz. amaretti cookies, plus 2 extra to decorate
3 tablespoons unsalted butter
3½ oz. dark chocolate (70% cocoa solids), chopped
¾ cup mascarpone
1 tablespoon confectioners' sugar
½ teaspoon vanilla extract
sifted cocoa powder, to dust

four 2½-inch diameter, loose-based tartlet pans

Serves 4

Put the apricots in a bowl, add sufficient boiling water to just cover, and leave to plump up until required.

Put the amaretti cookies in a polythene bag and bash to a fine crumb with a rolling pin. Melt the butter in a small saucepan, add the crumbed cookies and mix to combine.

Spoon this mixture into the tart pans and, using the back of a spoon, press down to cover the base and sides and create tart cases. Arrange on a tray or baking sheet and transfer to the fridge to chill and firm up.

Drain the apricots and mash them to a rough purée in a blender or using a handheld stick blender. You don't want a completely smooth purée; you want it to have some bits to give the tarts an interesting texture as well as taste.

Melt the chocolate in a heatproof bowl set over a saucepan of barely simmering water. Make sure the base of the bowl doesn't touch the water. Take off the heat and leave to cool for 5 minutes before folding in the mascarpone, confectioners' sugar, vanilla extract, and apricots.

Spoon the filling into the chilled tart cases. Either finish and serve immediately or chill until required, but let return to room temperature before serving.

To finish, crumble the extra amaretti cookies over the top of the tarts, dust with sifted cocoa powder and serve.

These tarts are best eaten on the day they are made.

MAKE MINE A MACCHIATO

These dinky mousses, in the style of macchiato espresso coffees topped with clouds of frothy milk, are the inspiration of Maisie, a good friend who is into her coffee and big flavors! Although ideally made with espresso coffee, this mousse will also work with good-quality instant coffee granules.

2½ oz. dark chocolate (minimum 70% cocoa solids), chopped
2 tablespoons dark brown sugar
1 tablespoon strong, freshly brewed espresso or 1 teaspoon instant coffee granules dissolved in 1 tablespoon boiling water
2 eggs, separated
2 oz. white chocolate, chopped
⅓ cup whipping cream

TO DECORATE
1 teaspoon roasted coffee beans
1 teaspoon roasted cocoa nibs

6–8 espresso cups, ramekins, or similar

Serves 6–8

Melt the dark chocolate in a heatproof bowl set over a pan of barely simmering water. Do not let the base of the bowl touch the water. Once melted, take the bowl off the heat and allow the chocolate to cool slightly.

Dissolve the dark brown sugar in the hot coffee and set aside to cool.

Lightly beat the egg yolks in a large bowl and add the cooled sugar and coffee mixture. Add the cooled melted chocolate and stir to combine. (Be careful not to "cook" the egg yolks with coffee or chocolate that is still too hot!)

Put the egg whites in a grease-free bowl and whisk until stiffly peaking. Gradually fold in the chocolate and egg yolk mixture using a large metal spoon.

Divide the mixture between the espresso cups, arrange on a tray or baking sheet and transfer to the fridge to set.

While the mousses are setting, melt the white chocolate in a heatproof bowl set over a saucepan of barely simmering water. Take the bowl off the heat and set aside to cool. Whip the

cream until just softly peaking. (Don't be tempted to whip it until stiff, as you want to create a soft layer to sit on top of the coffee mousse.) Gently fold the cooled melted white chocolate into the whipped cream and spoon on top of the chilled mousses.

Put the coffee beans, if using, in a mortar and crush with a pestle. Add the cocoa nibs, bash some more, and then sprinkle a little over the top of each mousse.

Serve immediately or chill until required, but let the mousses return to room temperature before serving.

These mousses can be covered and stored in the fridge for up to 2 days.

HONEYED RHUBARB CHOCOLATE FOOL

This is a lovely dessert to make in springtime, when rhubarb is in season and at its most delicious. Many thanks to Lucas Hollweg of *The Sunday Times* newspaper for giving me the inspiration to make a syrup, which allows the wonderful flavors of rhubarb, honey, and orange to sing, when blended into the chocolate fool.

1 lb. rhubarb, cut into
    2-inch lengths
finely grated peel of
    1 orange
freshly squeezed juice of
    ½ an orange
2 tablespoons clear honey
2 tablespoons superfine
    sugar (optional)
5½ oz. dark chocolate
    (minimum 70%
    cocoa solids), chopped
1¼ cups heavy cream
gingersnap cookies,
    to serve (optional)

a roasting pan

kitchen foil

*4–6 glass tumblers, sundae
dishes, or similar*

Serves 4–6

Preheat the oven to 350°F.

Put the rhubarb, grated orange peel and juice, and honey in the roasting pan and stir to ensure the rhubarb is well covered.

Cover the pan with foil and bake in the preheated oven for about 30 minutes, until the rhubarb is soft.

Strain the rhubarb juices into a saucepan. Transfer the fruit to a bowl and set aside to cool.

Taste the rhubarb juice and add the sugar only if you feel it needs sweetening. Set the saucepan over medium heat and bring the juice to a boil. Boil for at least 5 minutes, until syrupy.

Melt the chocolate in a heatproof bowl set over a saucepan of gently simmering water. Do not let the base of the bowl touch the water. Take off the heat and set aside to cool.

Whip the cream until softly peaking (don't be tempted to whip it until stiff, or the fool will be too firm once the chocolate is added). Stir in the cooled melted chocolate and 4 tablespoons of the rhubarb syrup. Add 2 tablespoons of the cooked rhubarb just to give it some texture.

To serve, spoon some rhubarb into each of the serving glasses, add a layer of chocolate fool, and finish with a layer of rhubarb, so that you get a lovely layered effect.

Drizzle any remaining rhubarb syrup over the top of the fools and serve immediately with gingersnap cookies, if liked.

A colorful, flavorsome Chococo version of a classic Italian dessert. Not only are these profiteroles made with chocolate, but they are filled with tangy fruit creams and drizzled with a hot chocolate sauce. The choux puffs keep for several days so can be made ahead and you can also vary the fruit creams to suit your taste and the seasons. Each quantity of cream will fill ten choux puffs so double up the quantities if you want to make just one flavor.

CHOCOLATE PROFITEROLE PYRAMID

CHOUX PASTRY
½ cup plus 1 tablespoon all-purpose flour
1 tablespoon cocoa powder
3 tablespoons unsalted butter, cut into pieces
2 eggs, beaten

BLACK CURRANT CREAM FILLING
1 cup fresh or frozen black currants
1 teaspoon light brown sugar
¼ cup whipping cream
1 teaspoon cassis (optional)
confectioners' sugar, to taste

MANGO CREAM FILLING
3½ oz. fresh mango flesh
½ teaspoon finely grated lime peel
¼ cup whipping cream

CHOCOLATE SAUCE
4½ oz. dark chocolate (minimum 65% cocoa solids), chopped
2 oz. semi-sweet chocolate (minimum 35% cocoa solids), chopped
⅓ cup just-boiled water

a baking sheet, greased and lined with baking parchment

a piping bag, fitted with a large round nozzle (optional)

Makes about 20 puffs

Preheat the oven to 425°F.

To make the choux pastry, sift the flour and cocoa onto a piece of baking parchment and place close to hand.

Put the butter in a heavy-based saucepan, add a scant ⅓ cup cold water and set over low heat. (The water must not come to a boil before the butter has melted, or it will evaporate and reduce the quantity of liquid you have for the choux dough.) When the butter has melted, increase the heat and bring to a boil. The moment it is boiling, remove the pan from the heat and, holding the paper like a funnel, quickly shoot the flour and cocoa powder into the pan.

Beat with a wooden spoon until smooth and glossy and keep mixing until the mixture forms a ball and leaves the sides of the pan clean. Let cool for 10 minutes before adding the egg a tablespoonful at a time, beating well after each addition. (You can use a handheld electric mixer to do this but I think you get a better feel for the choux dough if you beat it by hand.) You may not need to add all the egg—you are aiming for a dough that is thick, glossy, holds its shape well, and doesn't drop too easily from a spoon.

Spoon the dough into the prepared piping bag. (If you do not have a piping bag, you can make a simple bag with a polythene freezer bag. Spoon the dough into the bag, push it to one corner, and snip off the corner to create a small hole, about ½ inch.) Pipe (or squeeze) balls about the size of a large marble directly onto the prepared baking sheet.

Bake the choux puffs in the preheated oven for 10 minutes, then reduce the oven temperature to 350°F and bake for a further 15 minutes. They are ready when risen, have a crisp shell, and a hollow, moist interior. Remove the puffs from the oven and immediately pierce each one to allow the steam to escape. (This prevents the moisture inside turning them soggy.) Transfer the puffs to a wire rack and leave to cool before filling. If the puffs go soft, you can return them to a low oven for a few minutes just to crisp them up again.

To make the black currant cream filling, put the blackcurrants in a saucepan and add the sugar and 2 teaspoons cold water. Cook over low heat until the liquid starts to thicken. Set aside to cool. Whip the cream with a handheld electric mixer until stiffly peaking. Add the cooled blackcurrants, cassis (if using), and confectioners' sugar to taste. Cover and chill in the fridge until required.

To make the mango cream filling, put the mango and grated lime peel in a blender and process to a purée. Whip the cream with a handheld electric mixer until stiffly peaking. Stir in the mango purée and chill in the fridge until required.

To make the chocolate sauce, melt the chocolates in a heatproof bowl set over a pan of barely simmering water. When melted, gradually add the water, stirring continuously until you have a smooth pouring sauce.

When ready to serve, split the puffs and fill with the fruit creams using a teaspoon. Pile the puffs in a pyramid. Drizzle the hot chocolate sauce over the top and pour the rest of the sauce in a pitcher. Serve immediately.

SALTED CARAMEL PRALINE PAVLOVA

This is a pavlova with attitude, less ballet dancer, more high-energy hip hop. Not only is the meringue made with chocolate, but it is topped with a sour chocolate ganache studded with a crunchy salted caramel praline brittle, to both cut through the sweetness and also give you occasional and deliciously unexpected salt notes.

MERINGUE
3 egg whites
1 cup superfine sugar
1 tablespoon cocoa powder
2 teaspoons cornstarch
2 oz. dark chocolate (70% cocoa solids), grated
1 teaspoon white wine vinegar

SALTED PRALINE BRITTLE
½ cup plus 1 tablespoon granulated sugar
⅓ cup chopped hazelnuts
⅓ cup slivered almonds
¼ teaspoon sea salt

SOUR CHOCOLATE GANACHE
5½ oz. dark chocolate (70% cocoa solids)
½ cup sour cream
½ cup heavy cream
sifted cocoa powder, to dust

2 baking sheets, 1 lined with baking parchment marked with a 8-inch circle, 1 greased with a flavorless oil (such as grapeseed)

Serves 6–8

Preheat the oven to 350°F.

To make the meringue, put the egg whites in a grease-free bowl and whisk until softly peaking. Gradually add the sugar and continue whisking until you have a thick, glossy meringue that stands up in stiff peaks.

Sift the cocoa powder and cornstarch into the meringue. Add the grated chocolate and vinegar and using a large metal spoon, gently fold everything together to combine.

Spread the mixture out within the circle marked on the prepared lined baking sheet. Make an indentation in the center of the meringue. Put the meringue in the preheated oven but immediately reduce the temperature to 300°F. Bake for 1 hour, turn the oven off and leave the meringue in the oven until completely cold. (You can also make the meringue a few days ahead and keep it in an airtight container until required.)

To make the salted praline brittle, put the sugar in a heavy-based saucepan and set over low heat. Avoid stirring the sugar, but swirl the pan to spread the sugar around as it melts. Combine the hazelnuts and almonds and dry toast in a skillet. Reserve about 2 tablespoons

to use for decoration. Put the remaining toasted nuts into the caramelized sugar, add the sea salt and mix well. Spread the mixture out onto the prepared greased baking sheet. Leave to cool and set at room temperature. Once set, store in an airtight container until required.

To make the sour chocolate ganache, put the chocolate, ¼ cup of the sour cream and the heavy cream in a heatproof bowl set over a saucepan of barely simmering water. When melted, take off the heat and let cool before transferring to the fridge to chill for at least 1 hour.

When you are ready to serve, take the ganache out of the fridge and let it come to room temperature. Using a handheld electric mixer, whisk the ganache until soft and mousse-like. Chop the salted praline brittle into small pieces and stir into the ganache. Watch out though, if you add the brittle to the ganache too early it will start to melt and won't have it's pleasing crunch.

Put the meringue on a serving plate, top with the ganache mixture and the remaining sour cream, scatter over the reserved toasted nuts, and finish with a dusting of sifted cocoa powder. Serve in slices.

CHOCOLATE FONDUE WITH FROZEN CHERRIES

This dessert has a wonderful wow factor and couldn't be simpler to put together. It works on the principle that making a chocolate sauce with water means that it will stay liquid, even when very cold things are dipped into it. You can serve almost anything you like with your fondue—from fresh fruit to mini cookies, marshmallows, and biscotti—but my favorite accompaniment is fresh cherries frozen on their stalks. Dipping an ice-cold cherry into warm chocolate is certainly a sensory experience and always gets a reaction!

FONDUE

6 oz. dark chocolate (65–70% cocoa solids), chopped

2½ oz. semi-sweet chocolate (35% cocoa solids), chopped

½ cup just-boiled water

1 teaspoon vanilla extract, or a pinch of chili powder or ground cinnamon, to taste (optional)

FOR DIPPING

about 40 fresh cherries, stems intact

any seasonal fruits

1 quantity Mini Chili, Chocolate, & Cocoa Nib Cookies (see page 80)

biscotti

amaretti cookies

marshmallows

ice cube trays, sufficient to make 40 cubes

a fondue pot with burner and 6–8 fondue forks (optional)

Serves 6–8

To prepare the cherries, wash and pat dry with paper towels. Do not remove the stalks. Put one cherry in each hole in the ice cube trays. Transfer to the freezer and leave for at least 2 hours, until frosted and firm.

Take out of the freezer about 10 minutes before serving, so that they just start to defrost and take on a wonderful sheen.

To make the fondue, put the chocolates in a heatproof bowl set over a saucepan of barely simmering water and let melt gently. Do not let the base of the bowl touch the water.

Once the chocolate has melted pour in the just-boiled water, a third at a time, stirring after each addition, until you have a smooth sauce. (Do not add the water while it is still boiling as it may scorch the chocolate.)

Stir in the vanilla extract, chili powder, or cinnamon (if using). If the fondue seems too thick, add a little more hot (not boiling) water; if it's too thin and watery, add more chopped chocolate.

Leave the fondue in the bowl set over the saucepan of water, but turn the heat off if you are working ahead. You can always reheat the sauce just before serving, if necessary.

Arrange the frozen cherries and any other dipping treats of your choice on a large serving platter.

Pour the fondue into the fondue pot and light the burner to keep it warm. If you do not have a fondue set, warm a heatproof serving bowl in a low oven, pour the fondue into it and serve immediately.

To serve, provide fondue forks (if you don't have a fondue set, ordinary forks will work just as well) and plenty of napkins—a fondue can be a messy business but it's fun and always popular!

ICE CREAM
& sauces

HEAVENLY HONEYCOMB FUDGE SUNDAE

Life would be very dull without ice cream sundaes. We all think so at Chococo and a lot of our café customers who tuck into our Heavenly Honeycomb Fudge Sundaes would agree! I have included a simple recipe here for crunchy honeycomb but it can be quite tricky to make if you are not used to working with boiling sugar. If it doesn't work first time, don't give up on it—once you get the knack, it is quite a party trick!

16-oz. container premium vanilla ice cream, slightly softened
1 quantity Hot Fudge Sauce (see page 141)
½ cup whipping cream, whipped to stiff peaks
sugar-coated chocolate beans

HONEYCOMB
1 cup granulated sugar
5 tablespoons liquid glucose or corn syrup
1 tablespoon baking soda

a large baking sheet, lined with baking parchment

a sugar thermometer (optional)

4 glass sundae dishes

Serves 4

To make the honeycomb, put the sugar, glucose, and 3 tablespoons cold water in a large, heavy-based saucepan and set over low heat. Stir until the sugar has dissolved. Turn up the heat and boil at a high temperature for about 5 minutes, without stirring, until the sugar syrup reaches 315°F on a sugar thermometer. If you do not have a sugar thermometer, you can test whether the sugar syrup has reached the right temperature by dipping a teaspoon in the boiling sugar and then quickly putting it in a cup of cold water placed next to your pan. The sugar on the spoon will bubble and give a slight "crack" sound, which can sometimes be felt through the spoon. If the sugar is still not hot enough, continue to boil and test again a few minutes later. When ready, the sugar syrup will change to a richer golden color.

When the hard crack stage has been reached, you need to work fast. Simultaneously add the baking soda as you take the pan off the heat and begin whisking vigorously with a balloon whisk. The honeycomb will

foam up as you add the baking soda—be prepared for it to potentially quadruple in size as you whisk! Be aware that it is extremely hot. Keep whisking as you pour the foaming mixture onto the prepared baking sheet.

Leave to cool at room temperature (without touching) for about 20 minutes, until it has set. Once set, you can break it up into bite-size chunks or crumble it as required. Any left over will keep in an airtight container for up to 1 week.

To assemble the sundaes, put two scoops of ice cream in the bottom of each dish. Drizzle with a few tablespoonfuls of the hot fudge sauce and scatter with honeycomb chunks and some finer crumbs. Add a final scoop of ice cream and drizzle with more sauce. Top with a dollop of whipped cream and finish with more honeycomb and the chocolate beans sprinkled over the top.

Serve immediately, with long-handled sundae spoons if you have them.

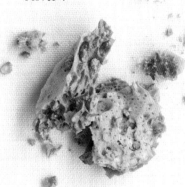

BRILLIANT BROWNIE

This is always a winner and one of our more popular treat plates served in our café. It can be made to suit any number of people, you just need to be a little bit organized and make all the elements required upfront and then, to use a chef's expression, "plate it up" just before serving.

2 brownie squares – choose from Squidgy Pecan Brownies (see page 64) or Cranberry and White Chocolate Brownies (see page 67)
2 scoops of premium ice cream (any flavor you like, but vanilla works well)
4–6 tablespoons warm sauce of your choice (see page 141)
2 swirls of whipped cream (optional)
fresh strawberries and/or raspberries, to serve
sifted confectioners' sugar, to dust (optional)

Serves 2

Warm the brownies in a low oven for a few minutes if necessary.

Place the brownies on serving plates. Put a generous scoop of ice cream on top of each one. Drizzle hot sauce over the ice cream and around the brownies.

If you want to make this an even more decadent taste experience, add a swirl of whipped cream to each plate.

Arrange a few strawberries and/or raspberries around the brownies, and dust the berries with a little sifted confectioners' sugar, only if they are tart and need a little sweetening.

Serve immediately.

LISELOTTE'S CHOCOLATE BLISS

This is the winning recipe in our Chococo customer competition, and was created by Susie Bond of Steeple, here in Purbeck, and her Swiss friend, Liselotte Bachmann. This is Susie's interpretation of one of Liselotte's favorite recipes, who describes it as the best chocolate dessert ever! It is best made the day before you want to serve it and is a truly decadent treat.

3½ oz. semi-sweet chocolate (35–40% cocoa solids), chopped
3 oz. dark chocolate (70% cocoa solids), chopped
6½ tablespoons unsalted butter, cut into pieces
4 eggs, separated
a pinch of salt
¼ teaspoon baking powder
4 tablespoons raw cane sugar
3 tablespoons single malt whisky or brandy
3½ oz. dark chocolate, made into curls or grated (see page 15)
light cream, to serve

an 8 x 4 x 2½-inch loaf pan, lined with foil or a baking parchment loaf tin liner

Serves 8–10

Put the semi-sweet and dark chocolates in separate heatproof bowls and set over saucepans of barely simmering water. Let melt, stirring intermittently with a spatula. Do not let the bases of the bowls touch the water.

When the chocolates have melted, remove the bowls from the heat. Divide the butter equally between the bowls and stir until it has melted.

Put the egg whites in a grease-free bowl. Add the salt and baking powder and, using a handheld electric mixer, whisk until softly peaking. Gradually add the sugar and continue whisking until the eggs stand up in firm peaks.

Mix 2 egg yolks into each bowl of melted chocolate and butter mixture and stir 1½ tablespoons of whisky into each one.

Divide the whisked egg whites between the 2 bowls and gently fold in with a metal spoon, ensuring that you blend all the chocolate and egg whites together.

Put dollops of each chocolate mousse into the prepared loaf pan, alternating the mixtures, to create a marbled effect.

Cover with plastic wrap and transfer to the freezer for a minimum of 5 hours, or ideally overnight.

Take out of the freezer about 10 minutes before serving. Turn out onto a platter and decorate with grated chocolate or chocolate curls.

Cut with a hot knife or cake slice to ensure clean slices and serve with a pitcher of chilled cream on the side for pouring.

NUTS ABOUT CHOCOLATE SUNDAE

The perfect dessert for all fans of chocolate, toffee and nuts, this rich sundae is full of texture and flavors. Chocolate and toffee ice creams are served with crunchy praline brittle, toasted nuts, and intensely flavored cocoa nibs and smothered in salted caramel sauce for a truly delicious taste experience.

½ cup macadamia nuts

½ cup whipping cream

16-oz. container premium chocolate ice cream, slightly softened

16-oz. container premium toffee ice cream, slightly softened

4 teaspoons roasted cocoa nibs (optional)

1 quantity Salted Caramel Sauce (see page 141)

4 long shards of Nuts About Nuts Praline Brittle Slabs (see page 31)

4 glass sundae dishes

Serves 4

Roughly chop the macadamia nuts and dry toast in a skillet until golden. Set aside until needed.

Whip the cream with an electric handheld mixer until stiffly peaking and put in the fridge until needed.

To assemble the sundaes, put a scoop of chocolate ice cream in the bottom of each dish. Add a little whipped cream and top with a scoop of toffee ice cream.

Sprinkle over half of the macadamia nuts and cocoa nibs (if using) and drizzle with a few spoonfuls of salted caramel sauce.

Add a second scoop of chocolate ice cream and drizzle over the remainder of the sauce.

Put a dollop of whipped cream on top of each sundae and scatter over the remaining macadamia nuts and cocoa nibs.

Stick a shard of praline brittle into the side of the sundae to finish, and serve immediately, with long-handled sundae spoons if you have them.

BAKED ALASKA CHOCOCO STYLE

1 Brownie Base
(see below)
3½ oz. dark chocolate
(70% cocoa solids),
chopped
a handful of pop rocks
candy (optional)
1 cup fresh raspberries
1 tablespoon framboise
or brandy (optional)
3 egg whites
¼ teaspoon cream
of tartar
1 teaspoon vanilla extract
½ cup superfine sugar
4 scoops of premium
vanilla ice cream
sifted cocoa powder,
to dust

BROWNIE BASE
5½ oz. dark chocolate
(70% cocoa solids),
chopped
6½ tablespoons unsalted
butter, cut into pieces
2 eggs, beaten
½ cup packed light
brown sugar
½ teaspoon vanilla
extract
⅓ cup fine rice flour
¼ teaspoon sea salt

*a 9-inch square baking
pan, lined with foil*

*2 baking sheets, lined with
baking parchment*

*a 3-inch diameter round
cutter*

*a cook's blowtorch,
(optional)*

Serves 4

Preheat the oven to 325°F.

To make the brownie base, put the chocolate and butter in a heatproof bowl set over a pan of barely simmering water. When melted, take off the heat and let cool for a few minutes.

Beat the eggs, sugar, and vanilla extract together in a large bowl using a handheld electric mixer, until light and mousse-like. Fold in the rice flour and salt. Add the melted chocolate and butter mixture and gently fold everything together. Pour the chocolate brownie mixture into the prepared baking pan and tap it on the work surface to ensure it is level.

Bake in the preheated oven for about 15 minutes, until risen at the edges but still squidgy in the middle. Leave the brownie to cool completely in the pan.

To make the chocolate disks, melt the chocolate slowly in a heatproof bowl set over a pan of barely simmering water. Do not let the base of the bowl touch the water.

While the chocolate is melting, draw 4 circles on one of the lined baking sheets, using the cutter as a template. Put a dessertspoonful of melted chocolate into each circle and spread out with the back of the spoon to fill the space. Sprinkle a little pop rocks candy (if using) over each disk. Transfer the baking sheet to the fridge and leave the chocolate disks to set.

To assemble the baked alaskas, put the cooled brownie base on a flat surface and use the cutter to stamp out 4 rounds. Use a fish slice to transfer each round to the second lined baking sheet. Leave some space between the brownies so that you have room to work.

Top each brownie round with a layer of raspberries. Drizzle a little framboise or brandy over the fruit (if using). Put a chilled chocolate disk on top of the raspberries and then put the baking sheet in the fridge until required.

Preheat the oven to 450°F or prepare a cook's blowtorch if you have one.

Take the ice cream out of the freezer now to give it time to soften. Put the egg whites in a grease-free bowl and whisk with a handheld electric mixer until softly peaking. Mix in the cream of tartar and vanilla extract then gradually whisk in the sugar until stiff peaks form.

Working very quickly, assemble the baked alaskas. Put a scoop of ice cream on each raspberry and chocolate disk-topped brownie base and cover each with the meringue mixture. Use a palette knife to swirl it around and seal everything inside the meringue. Either bake immediately in the preheated oven for just 3–4 minutes, until the meringue is golden brown. Alternatively, use a cook's blowtorch to brown the meringue.

Dust lightly with sifted cocoa powder and serve immediately.

This is a bit retro but always such fun to serve. I went through a bit of a baked alaska phase in my student days, although I do have memories of sometimes being slightly worse for wear by the time dessert was required and not getting the oven temperatures quite hot enough… so my top tip is that this is not a dessert to attempt unless very sober! I have used a squidgy chocolate brownie base and hidden a layer of crisp chocolate inside to make these individual alaskas an extra special treat.

A SAUCY PAGE...

I believe that there is a sauce for every occasion—from the "this dessert deserves a truly decadent sauce to go with it", to "I haven't got any fresh cream in the fridge but I still have a hot chocolate sauce itch to scratch", to the "can we have a sundae?!" yell from the kids...you get the idea. These recipes can all be easily doubled up or even quadrupled if you are catering for a small army.

POSH CHOCOLATE SAUCE

3 oz. dark chocolate (70% cocoa solids), chopped
²⁄₃ cup light cream
1 tablespoon milk
½ tablespoon light brown sugar

2 tablespoons unsalted butter
a little warmed milk, to thin, if required

Makes 4–6 servings

Put the chocolate, cream, milk, and sugar in a heavy-based saucepan and set over a gentle heat. Melt, stirring continuously, until the butter has melted and you have a smooth, glossy sauce. If you would like it to be a little runnier, simply add a little warmed milk. Check the sweetness at this point, adding more sugar to taste.

SALTED CARAMEL SAUCE

⅓ cup packed light brown sugar
1 cup heavy cream
1 tablespoon unsalted butter

½ teaspoon vanilla extract
½ teaspoon sea salt (optional)

Makes 6 servings

This is a very easy sauce to make—just put all of the ingredients in a small heavy-based saucepan and set over low heat. Stir as they melt together, then bring to a boil and let boil gently for about 5 minutes, until the sauce thickens. Don't serve it immediately though, as it will be very hot!

WATER-BASED CHOCOLATE SAUCE

4 oz. dark chocolate (70% cocoa solids), chopped
2 oz. milk chocolate

(35% cocoa solids), chopped
½ cup just-boiled water

Makes 4–6 servings

Put the two chocolates in a heatproof bowl set over a saucepan of barely simmering water. When melted, gradually add the water, stirring continuously until you have a smooth sauce. If you feel it is too thick, add a little more hot water, if too thin, add more chopped chocolate and let it melt in.

HOT FUDGE SAUCE

2½ oz. dark chocolate (65% cocoa solids), chopped
3½ tablespoons unsalted butter
¼ cup cocoa powder

½ cup packed light brown sugar
⅓ cup heavy cream
⅓ cup milk

Makes 6 servings

Put the chocolate and butter in a bowl set over a saucepan of barely simmering water. When melted, take the bowl off the heat, sift in the cocoa powder whisk until dissolved. Warm the milk and cream in a saucepan and add the sugar. Bring to a boil and cook for a few minutes, stirring occasionally, until the sugar has dissolved. Take off the heat and gradually add the hot cream mixture to chocolate mixture, stirring constantly. It might be a bit lumpy to start with but as you add more liquid, it will turn into a smooth sauce.

INDEX

conversion chart

Volume equivalents:

American	Metric	Imperial
6 tbsp butter	85 g	3 oz.
7 tbsp butter	100 g	$3\frac{1}{2}$ oz.
1 stick butter	115 g	4 oz.
1 teaspoon	5 ml	
1 tablespoon	15 ml	
$\frac{1}{4}$ cup	60 ml	2 fl.oz.
$\frac{1}{3}$ cup	75 ml	$2\frac{1}{2}$ fl.oz.
$\frac{1}{2}$ cup	125 ml	4 fl.oz.
$\frac{2}{3}$ cup	150 ml	5 fl.oz. ($\frac{1}{4}$ pint)
$\frac{3}{4}$ cup	175 ml	6 fl.oz.
1 cup	250 ml	8 fl.oz.

Oven temperatures:

170°C	(325°F)	Gas 3
180°C	(350°F)	Gas 4
190°C	(375°F)	Gas 5
200°C	(400°F)	Gas 6
220°C	(425°F)	Gas 8

Weight equivalents:

Imperial	Metric
1 oz.	30 g
2 oz.	55 g
3 oz.	85 g
$3\frac{1}{2}$ oz.	100 g
4 oz.	115 g
5 oz.	140 g
6 oz.	175 g
8 oz. ($\frac{1}{2}$ lb.)	225 g
9 oz.	250 g
10 oz.	280 g
$11\frac{1}{2}$ oz.	325 g
12 oz.	350 g
13 oz.	375 g
14 oz.	400 g
15 oz.	425 g
16 oz. (1 lb.)	450 g

Measurements:

Inches	Cm
$\frac{1}{4}$ inch	0.5 cm
$\frac{1}{2}$ inch	1 cm
$\frac{3}{4}$ inch	1.5 cm
1 inch	2.5 cm
2 inches	5 cm
3 inches	7 cm
4 inches	10 cm
5 inches	12 cm
6 inches	15 cm
7 inches	18 cm
8 inches	20 cm
9 inches	23 cm
10 inches	25 cm
11 inches	28 cm
12 inches	30 cm

ACKNOWLEDGMENTS

This book wouldn't have happened without the support of my husband Andy who, by agreeing to run with my crazy idea to set up Chococo in the first place, has ended up living a life he never expected and who has worked so tirelessly ever since to make it what it is today. I also want to thank our brilliant team at Chococo for their hard work, commitment, and passion for our business. Big thanks also to our children, Lily and Max, for putting up so patiently with a constantly busy mummy and for their (messy) enthusiasm in the kitchen; to my mum and dad Sandra and David Allpress; to David and Paddy Price-Hughes for all the boxes and babysitting; to my chief testers, Becs Meteau, Maisie Gawler-Wright, and Sarah Aspinall for their creativity and inspiring input; and the rest of my testing crew: Evelyn Hoy (Northern Irish peace issues were put to one side for a while to focus on baking), Juliet Boyd, my sister Frances Clark and her friends in Dublin, Janice Edgar, Louise Stewart, Kay Jenkins, Anna Waymouth, and her sons Jack and Alfie, Emily Aspinall, and Minna Gawler-Wright. I also want to thank all our shop and café customers and my book group for eating my test batches and for giving me such honest feedback! Many thanks to Steph Shepherd of the Lobster Pot Beach Café and Matt of the Winterborne Bakery for contributing their recipes, to all our suppliers including Trevor Craig of Craig's Farm Dairy; Tony, Carl, and the team at HB ingredients; beekeeper Robert Field; Janet Pook, Sue, and Kim of Peasant Products and all the Dorset food producers who have been so supportive of our endeavours over the years.

Thanks, too, to Karen Welman of Pearlfisher for her inspirational design and encouragement from pre-launch of Chococo; Toby Hampton for all his PR expertise; Sara Jayne Stanes, Sarah Jane Evans, Paul A Young, Chantal Coady, and everyone at the Academy of Chocolate for their support; Alison Starling, Julia Charles, Leslie Harrington, and Megan Smith of Ryland Peters & Small for their endless patience with me; Jonathon Gregson for his brilliant photography; Joss Herd for her beautiful food styling; and Clare Hulton my agent, for badgering me to think about writing a book in the first place, after spotting us in our pink gazebo at Camp Bestival in 2009!

Finally, I would like to thank Sir Chay Blyth and Pete Goss for teaching me a very important life lesson when I trained for the BT Global Challenge Round the World yacht race back in 1996/7; namely that "persistence and determination are omnipotent."

6/15